IN SEARCH OF A
UNIVERSAL ETHIC:
A NEW LOOK AT THE NATURAL LAW

INTERNATIONAL THEOLOGICAL COMMISSION

*All documents are published thanks to the generous support
of the members of the Catholic Truth Society*

CATHOLIC TRUTH SOCIETY
PUBLISHERS TO THE HOLY SEE

CONTENTS

INTRODUCTION

1. Are there objective moral values which can unite human beings and bring them peace and happiness? What are they? How are they discerned? How can they be put into action in the lives of persons and communities? These perennial questions concerning good and evil are today more urgent than ever, insofar as people have become more aware of forming one single world community. The great problems that arise for human beings today have an international, worldwide dimension, inasmuch as advances in communications technology have given rise to closer interaction among individuals, societies and cultures. A local event can have an almost immediate worldwide repercussion. The consciousness of global solidarity is thus emerging, which finds its ultimate foundation in the unity of the human race. This finds expression in the sense of planetary responsibility. Thus, the question of ecological balance, of the protection of the environment, resources and climate, has become a pressing preoccupation faced by all humanity, and whose solution extends far beyond national boundaries. Likewise, threats of terrorism, organized crime and new forms of violence and oppression that weigh upon societies have a global dimension. The accelerated developments of biotechnologies, which sometimes threaten the very identity of man (genetic manipulation, cloning ...), urgently call for an ethical and political reflection of a universal breadth. In this context, the search for common ethical values experiences a revival of relevance.

2. By their wisdom, their generosity and sometimes their heroism, men and women give active witness to these common ethical values. Our admiration for such people is a sign of a spontaneous initial grasp of moral values. Academic and scientific reflection on the cultural, political, economic, moral and religious dimensions of our social existence nourishes this reflection on the common good of humanity. There are also artists who, by the manifestation of beauty, react against the loss of meaning and give renewed hope to men and women. Likewise, some politicians work with energy and creativity to put programs into place for the elimination of poverty and the protection of fundamental freedoms. Very important also is the constant witness of the representatives of religions and spiritual traditions who

wish to live by the light of the ultimate truth and the absolute good. All contribute, each in his own manner and in a reciprocal exchange, to the promotion of peace, a more just political order, the sense of common responsibility, an equitable distribution of riches, as well as respect for the environment, for the dignity of the human person and his fundamental rights. However, these efforts cannot succeed unless good intentions rest on a solid foundational agreement regarding the goods and values that represent the most profound aspirations of man, both as an individual and as member of a community. Only the recognition and promotion of these ethical values can contribute to the construction of a more human world.

3. The search for this common ethical language concerns everyone. For Christians, it is mysteriously in harmony with the work of the Word of God, "the true light that enlightens every man" (*Jn* 1:9), and with the work of the Holy Spirit who knows how to germinate in hearts "love, joy, peace, patience, kindness, goodness, faithfulness, gentleness, self-control" (*Gal* 5:22-23). The community of Christians, which shares "the joys and hopes, the griefs and the anxieties of the men of this age" and "therefore experiences itself really and intimately in solidarity with mankind and its history"[1], cannot in any way hide from this common responsibility. Enlightened by the Gospel, engaged in a patient and respectful dialogue with all persons of good will, Christians participate in the common endeavour to promote human values: "Whatever is true, whatever is honorable, whatever is just, whatever is pure, whatever is lovely, whatever is gracious, if there is any excellence, if there is anything worthy of praise, think about these things" (*Phil* 4:8). They know that Jesus Christ, "our peace" (*Eph* 2:14), who has reconciled all human beings to God by his cross, is the principle of the most profound unity towards whom the human race is called to converge.

4. The search for a common ethical language is inseparable from an experience of conversion, by which persons and communities turn away from the forces that seek to imprison them in indifference or cause them to raise walls against the other and against the stranger. The heart of

---

[1] VATICAN COUNCIL II, Pastoral constitution *Gaudium et spes*, preface, n. 1.

stone – cold, inert and indifferent to the lot of one's neighbor and of the human race – must be transformed, under the action of the Spirit, into a heart of flesh[2], sensitive to wisdom that calls us to compassion, to the desire for peace and hope for all. This conversion is the condition for true dialogue.

5. Contemporary attempts to define a universal ethic are not lacking. Shortly after the Second World War, the community of nations, seeing the consequences of the close collusion that totalitarianism had maintained with pure juridical positivism, defined in the *Universal Declaration of Human Rights* (1948) some inalienable rights of the human person. These rights transcend the positive law of states and must serve them both as a reference and a norm. These rights are not simply bestowed by a lawmaker: they are declared, which is to say, their objective existence, prior to any decision of the lawmaker, is made manifest. They flow, in fact, from the "recognition of the inherent dignity…of all members of the human family" (Preamble).

The *Universal Declaration of Human Rights* constitutes one of the most beautiful successes of modern history. It "remains one of the highest expressions of human conscience in our times"[3], and it offers a solid basis for promoting a more just world. Nevertheless, the results have not always been as high as the hopes. Certain countries have contested the universality of these rights, judged to be too Western, prompting a search for a more comprehensive formulation. Moreover, a certain propensity towards multiplying human rights more according to the disordered desires of the consumerist individual or the demands of interest groups, rather than the objective requirements of the common good of humanity, has – in no small way – contributed to their devaluation. Disconnected from the moral sense of values, which transcend particular interests, the multiplication of procedures and juridical regulations leads into a quagmire, which, when all is said and done, only serves the interests of the most powerful. Above all, a tendency comes to the fore to reinterpret human rights, separating them from the ethical and rational

---

[2] Cf. Ezek 36:26.

[3] JOHN PAUL II, *Address of October 5, 1995 to the General Assembly of the United Nations for the celebration of the 50th anniversary of its founding* (*Insegnamenti di Giovanni Paolo II* 18,2 [1995], p. 732).

dimension that constitutes their foundation and their end, in favor of pure utilitarian legalism[4].

6. In order to make explicit the ethical foundation of human rights, some have tried to elaborate a "global ethic" in the framework of a dialogue between cultures and religions. The "global ethic" refers to the collection of fundamental obligatory values which for centuries have formed the patrimony of human experience. It is found in all the great religious and philosophical traditions[5]. This project, worthy of interest, is indicative of the current need for an ethic possessing universal and global validity. But does a purely inductive search, conducted on the parliamentary model, for an already existing minimal consensus, satisfy the requirements for basing law on what is absolute? Moreover, does not this minimal ethic lead to relativizing the strong ethical requirements of each of the religions or particular schools of wisdom?

---

[4] Cf. BENEDICT XVI, *Address of April 18, 2008 before the General Assembly of the United Nations Organization in New York* in (AAS 100 [2008], p 335): "The merit of the *Universal Declaration* is that it has enabled different cultures, juridical expressions and institutional models to converge around a fundamental nucleus of values, and hence of rights. Today, though, efforts need to be redoubled in the face of pressure to reinterpret the foundations of the *Declaration* and to compromise its inner unity so as to facilitate a move away from the protection of human dignity towards the satisfaction of simple interests, often particular interests. ... Experience shows that legality often prevails over justice when the insistence upon rights makes them appear as the exclusive result of legislative enactments or normative decisions taken by the various agencies of those in power. When presented purely in terms of legality, rights risk becoming weak propositions divorced from the ethical and rational dimension which is their foundation and their goal. The *Universal Declaration*, rather, has reinforced the conviction that respect for human rights is principally rooted in unchanging justice, on which the binding force of international proclamations is also based. This aspect is often overlooked when the attempt is made to deprive rights of their true function in the name of a narrowly utilitarian perspective".

[5] In 1993, some representatives of the Parliament of the World's Religions published a *Declaration Toward a Global Ethic* which states that "there already exists among religions a consensus capable of founding a global ethic, a minimum consensus concerning binding values, irrevocable norms, and essential moral attitudes". This *Declaration* contains four principles. (1) "There is no new global order without a new global ethic". (2) "Every human being must be treated humanely". Taking human dignity into account is considered as an end in itself. This principle takes up the "golden rule" that is found in many religious traditions. (3) The *Declaration* enunciates four irrevocable moral directives: non-violence and respect for life; solidarity; tolerance and truth; equality between men and women. (4) Regarding the problems of humanity, a change of mentality is necessary, so that each one becomes aware of his urgent responsibility. It is a duty of the religions to cultivate this responsibility, to deepen it, and to hand it on to future generations.

8

7. For several decades, the question of the ethical foundations of law and politics has been set aside in certain sectors of contemporary culture. Under the pretext that every claim to possess an objective and universal truth would be the source of intolerance and violence, and that only relativism can safeguard the pluralism of values and democracy, a juridical positivism is espoused, which renounces any reference to an objective ontological criterion of what is just. In this perspective, the final horizon of law and the moral norm is the law in force, which is considered to be just by definition since it is the will of the legislator. But this opens the way to the arbitrary use of power, to the dictatorship of the numerical majority and to ideological manipulation, which harm the common good. "In today's ethics and philosophy of law, the postulates of juridical positivism are widespread. As a result, legislation often only becomes a compromise among different interests: one seeks to transform into law private interests or desires that are opposed to the duties flowing from social responsibility"[6]. But juridical positivism is notoriously insufficient, for a legislator can only act legitimately within certain limits, which derive from the dignity of the human person, and in service to the development of what is authentically human. Now, the legislator cannot abandon the determination of what is human to extrinsic and superficial criteria, as would be the case, for example, if he were to legalize, on his own, everything that is possible in the realm of biotechnology. In brief, he must act in an ethically responsible manner. Politics cannot cut itself off from ethics nor can civil laws and the juridical order prescind from a higher moral law.

8. In this context in which reference to absolute objective values, universally recognized, has become problematic, some people, wishing nevertheless to give a rational basis to common ethical decisions, advocate "discourse ethics" in keeping with a "dialogical" understanding of morality. Discourse ethics consists in using, in the course of ethical debate, only norms to which all the concerned participants – renouncing "strategies" aimed at imposing their own views – can give their assent. In this way, one can determine if a rule of conduct and action, or a specific behaviour is moral because, by bracketing off cultural and historical

---

[6] BENEDICT XVI, *Address of February 12, 2007 to the International Congress on Natural Moral Law organized by the Pontifical Lateran University* (AAS 99 [2007], p. 244).

conditioning, the principle of discussion offers a guarantee of universality and rationality. Discourse ethics is above all interested in a method by which, thanks to debate, ethical principles and norms can be tested and become obligatory for all the participants. It is essentially a process for testing the value of proposed norms, but it cannot produce new substantial contents. Discourse ethics is, therefore, a purely formal ethic that does not concern fundamental moral orientations. It also runs the risk of limiting itself to the search for compromise. Certainly, dialogue and debate are always necessary for obtaining an achievable agreement on the concrete application of moral norms in any given situation, but they should not relegate moral conscience to the margins. A true debate does not replace personal moral convictions, but it presupposes and enriches them.

9. Aware of what is currently at stake in the question, we would like, in this document, to invite all those pondering the ultimate foundations of ethics and of the juridical and political order, to consider the resources that a renewed presentation of the doctrine of the natural law contains. This law, in substance, affirms that persons and human communities are capable, in the light of reason, of discerning the fundamental orientations of moral action in conformity with the very nature of the human subject and of expressing these orientations in a normative fashion in the form of precepts or commandments. These fundamental precepts, objective and universal, are called upon to establish and inspire the collection of moral, juridical and political determinations that govern the life of human beings and societies. They constitute a permanent critical instance of them and guarantee the dignity of the human person in the face of the fluctuations of ideologies. In the course of its history, in the elaboration of its own ethical tradition, the Christian community, guided by the Spirit of Jesus Christ and in critical dialogue with the wisdom traditions it has encountered, has assumed, purified and developed this teaching on the natural law as a fundamental ethical norm. But Christianity does not have the monopoly on the natural law. In fact, founded on reason, common to all human beings, the natural law is the basis of collaboration among all persons of good will, whatever their religious convictions.

10. It is true that the term "natural law" is a source of numerous misunderstandings in our present cultural context. At times, it evokes only a resigned and completely passive submission to the physical laws of

nature, while human beings seek instead – and rightly so – to master and to direct these elements for their own good. At times, when presented as an objective datum that would impose itself from the outside on personal conscience, independently of the work of reason and subjectivity, it is suspected of introducing a form of heteronomy intolerable for the dignity of the free human person. Sometimes also, in the course of history, Christian theology has too easily justified some anthropological positions on the basis of the natural law, which subsequently appeared as conditioned by the historical and cultural context. But a more profound understanding of the relationships between the moral subject, nature and God, as well as a better consideration of the historicity that affects the concrete applications of the natural law, help to overcome these misunderstandings. It is likewise important today to set out the traditional doctrine of the natural law in terms that better manifest the personal and existential dimension of the moral life. It is also necessary to insist more on the fact that the expression of the requirements of the natural law is inseparable from the effort of the total human community to transcend egotistical and partisan tendencies and develop a global approach of the "ecology of values" without which human life risks losing its integrity and its sense of responsibility for the good of all.

11. The idea of the natural law takes on numerous elements that are common to humanity's great wisdom traditions, both religious and philosophical. In chapter 1, therefore, our document begins by evoking "convergences". Without pretending to be exhaustive, it indicates that these great religious and philosophical wisdom traditions bear witness to a largely common moral patrimony that forms the basis of all dialogue on moral questions. Even more, these suggest, in one way or another, that this patrimony reveals a universal ethical message inherent in the nature of things, which everyone is capable of discerning. The document then calls to mind several essential milestones in the historical development of the idea of the natural law and mentions certain modern interpretations that are partially at the origin of the difficulties that our contemporaries have concerning this notion. In chapter 2 ("The perception of common moral values"), our document describes how, beginning with the most basic data of moral experience, the human person immediately apprehends certain fundamental moral goods and formulates, as a result, the precepts of the natural law. These do not constitute a code entirely made of

intangible prescriptions but a permanent and normative guiding principle in the service of the concrete moral life of the person. Chapter 3 ("The foundations of the natural law"), passing from common experience to theory, deepens the philosophical, metaphysical and religious foundations of the natural law. In order to respond to some contemporary objections, it specifies the role of nature in personal action and inquires into the possibility of nature constituting a moral norm. Chapter 4 ("Natural Law and the City") makes explicit the regulating role of natural law precepts in political life. The doctrine of the natural law already possesses coherence and validity on the philosophical level of reason, common to all human beings, but chapter 5 ("Jesus Christ, the fulfillment of the natural law") shows that it acquires its full meaning within the history of salvation: sent by the Father, Jesus Christ is, in fact, by his Spirit, the fullness of all law.

CHAPTER 1: CONVERGENCES

1.1. The wisdom traditions and religions of the world

12. In diverse cultures, people have progressively elaborated and developed traditions of wisdom in which they express and transmit their vision of the world as well as their thoughtful perception of the place that man holds in society and the cosmos. Before all conceptual theorizing, these wisdom traditions, which are often of a religious nature, convey an experience that identifies what favors and what hinders the full blossoming of personal life and the smooth running of social life. They constitute a type of "cultural capital" available in the search for a common wisdom necessary for responding to contemporary ethical challenges. According to the Christian faith, these traditions of wisdom, in spite of their limitations and sometimes even their errors, capture a reflection of the divine wisdom at work in the hearts of human beings. They call for attention and respect, and can have value as a *praeparatio evangelica*.

The form and extent of these traditions can vary considerably. Nevertheless, they testify to the existence of a patrimony of moral values common to all human beings, no matter how these values are justified within a particular worldview. For example, the "golden rule" ("And what you hate, do not do to anyone" [*Tob* 4:15]) is found in one form or another in the majority of wisdom traditions[7]. Furthermore, these traditions generally agree in recognizing that the great ethical rules not only impose themselves on a specific human group, but also hold true for each individual and for all peoples. In fact, several traditions recognize that these universal moral behaviours are demanded by the very nature of man: they express the manner by which he is to enter, in a creative and harmonious way, into a cosmic or metaphysical order that transcends him and gives meaning to his life. This order is, in fact, filled with an immanent wisdom. It carries a moral message that human beings are capable of discerning.

---

[7] Cf St. Augustine, *De doctrina christiana*, III, xiv, 22 (*Corpus christianorum*, series latina, 32, p. 91): "The precept: "what you do not want done to yourself, do not do to another" cannot in any way differ according to the diversity of peoples ("Quod tibi fieri non vis, alii ne feceris", nullo modo posse ulla eorum gentili diversitate variari)". Cf. L. J. Philippidis, *Die "Goldene Rege" religionsgeschichtlich Untersucht* (Leipzig, 1929); A. Dihle, Die *Goldene Regel. Eine Einfuhrung in die Geschichte der antiken und fruhchristlichen Vulgarethik* (Gottingen, 1962); J. Wattles, *The Golden Rule* (New York: Oxford, 1996).

13

13. In the Hindu traditions, the world – the cosmos as well as human societies – is regulated by an order or fundamental law (*dharma*), which one must respect in order not to cause serious imbalances. *Dharma* then defines the socio-religious obligations of man. In its specificity, the moral teaching of Hinduism is understood in the light of the fundamental doctrines of the *Upanishads*: belief in an indefinite cycle of transmigrations (*samsāra*), with the idea that good and bad actions committed during the present life (*karman*) have an influence on successive rebirths. These doctrines have important consequences for one's behaviour with respect to others: they entail a high degree of goodness and tolerance, a sense of disinterested action for the benefit of others, as well as the practice of non-violence (*ahimsā*). The principal current of Hinduism distinguishes between two bodies of texts: *śruti* ("that which is understood", namely, revelation) and smrti ("that which one remembers", namely, tradition). The ethical prescriptions are especially found in the smrti, most particularly in the *dharmaśātra* (of which the most important is the *mānava dharmaśātra* or laws of Manu, ca. 200-100 B.C.). Besides the basic principle according to which "the immemorial custom is the transcendent law approved by sacred scripture and the codes of the divine legislators (consequently, all men of the three principal classes, who respect the supreme spirit that is in them, must always conform themselves with diligence to the immemorial custom")[8], one also finds an equivalent practice of the golden rule: "I will tell you what is the essence of the greatest good of the human being. The man who practices the religion (*dharma*) of do no harm to anyone without exception (*ahimsā*) acquires the greatest good. This man is the master of the three passions: cupidity, anger and avarice, and renouncing them in relation to all that exists, acquires success. ... This man who considers all creatures like 'himself' and treats them as his own 'self', laying down the punishing rod and dominating his anger completely, assures for himself the attainment of happiness. ... One will not do to another what one considers harmful to oneself. This, in brief, is the rule of virtue. ... In refusing and in giving, in abundance and in misery, in the agreeable and the disagreeable, one will judge all the consequences by considering one's own 'self'"[9].

---

[8] *Mānava dharmaśāthtra*, 1, 108 (G. C. Haughton, *Mānava Dharma śāstra or The Institutes of Manu*, Comprising the Indian System of Duties, Religious and Civil, ed. By P. Percival, New Delhi, 1982(4), 14.

[9] *Mahābhārata, Anusasana parva*, 113, 3-9 (ed. Ishwar Chundra Sharma and O. N. Bimali; translation according to M. N. Dutt [Parimal Publications, Delhi], vol. IX, p. 469).

Several precepts of the Hindu tradition can be placed in parallel with the requirements of the Decalogue[10].

14. One generally defines Buddhism by the four "noble truths" taught by the Buddha after his enlightenment: 1) reality is suffering and lack of satisfaction; 2) the origin of suffering is desire; 3) the cessation of suffering is possible (by the extinction of desire); 4) a way exists leading to the cessation of suffering. This way is the "noble eightfold path" which consists in the practice of discipline, concentration and wisdom. On the ethical level, the favorable actions can be summarized in the five precepts (*sila, sīla*): 1) do not injure living beings nor take away life; 2) do not take what is not given; 3) do not engage in immoral sexual conduct; 4) do not use false or lying words; 5) do not ingest intoxicating products that diminish mastery over oneself. The profound altruism of the Buddhist tradition, which is expressed in a resolute attitude of non-violence, amicable benevolence and compassion, thus agrees with the golden rule.

15. Chinese civilization is profoundly marked by the Taoism of Lǎozǐ or Lao-Tse (or Tzu) (6th century B.C.). According to Lao-Tse, the Way or Dào is the primordial principle, immanent within the entire universe. It is an indiscernible principle of permanent change under the action of two contrary and complementary poles, the *yīn* and the *yáng*. It is up to man to espouse this natural process of transformation, to let himself go in the flux of time by means of the attitude of non-action (*wú-wéi*). The search for harmony with nature, inseparably material and spiritual, is thus at the heart of the Taoist ethic. As for Confucius (551-479 B.C.), "Master Kong", he attempts, on the occasion of a period of profound crisis, to restore order by respect for rites, founded on filial piety that must be at the heart of all social life. Social relations, in fact, take family relations as their model. Harmony is obtained by an ethic of the happy mean, in which the ritualized relation (the *li*), which places man into the natural order, is the measure of all things. The ideal to be attained is *ren*, the perfect virtue of humanity, achieved by self-control and benevolence towards others.

---

[10] For example: "Let him say what is true, let him say what is pleasing, let him declare no disagreeable truth, and let him utter no lie to please someone; such is the eternal law" (*Mānava dharmaśāstra*, 4, 138, p. 101); "Let him always consider the action of striking a blow, reviling, and harming the good of one's neighbour, as the three most pernicious things in the string of vices produced by wrath" (*Mānava dharmaśāstra*, 7, 51, p. 156).

"'Reciprocity (*shù*)': is not this the key word? That which you would not wish done to you, do not do to others"[11]. The practice of this rule expresses the way of heaven (*Tiān Dào*).

16. In the African traditions, the fundamental reality is life itself. It is the most precious good, and the ideal of man consists not only in living to old age sheltered from cares, but most of all in remaining, even after death, a vital power continually reinforced and vivified in and by his progeny. Life is, in fact, a dramatic experience. Man, the microcosm at the heart of the macrocosm, intensely lives the drama of the confrontation between life and death. The mission that falls to him of assuring the victory of life over death, orients and determines his ethical action. In a consistent and rational ethical horizon, man, therefore, must identify the allies of life, win them to his cause and thus assure his survival that is, at the same time, the victory of life. Such is the profound meaning of traditional African religions. The African ethic thus manifests itself as an anthropocentric and vital ethic: the acts deemed favorable to the opening up of life, to conserving, protecting and causing it to flourish or to increasing the vital potential of the community, are, because of this, considered good; every act presumed prejudicial to the life of individuals or the community is judged to be bad. Traditional African religions thus appear to be essentially anthropocentric, but attentive observation coupled with reflection shows that neither the place accorded to the living man nor the cult of the ancestors constitutes something closed. The traditional African religions attain their highest point in God, the source of life, the creator of all that exists.

17. Islam understands itself as the restoration of the original natural religion. It sees in Muhammad the last prophet sent by God to put human beings definitively back on the right path. But Muhammad has been preceded by others: "For there is no community in which an 'admonisher' has not appeared"[12]. Islam, therefore, ascribes to itself a universal vocation and addresses itself to all human beings, who are considered as "naturally" Muslims. Islamic law, inseparably communitarian, moral and religious, is understood as a law directly given by God. The Islamic ethic is, therefore, fundamentally a morality of obedience. To do good is to

---

[11] Confucius, *Analects* 15, 23.

[12] *Koran,* sura 35, 24; cf. sura 13, 7.

obey the commandments; to do evil is to disobey them. Human reason intervenes to recognize the revealed character of the law and to derive from it the concrete juridical implications . To be sure, in the 9th century, the Mu'tazilite school proclaimed the idea that "good and evil are in things", which is to say, that certain behaviour is good or bad in itself, prior to the divine law that commands or forbids it. The Mu'tazilites, therefore, judged that man could by his reason know what is good and evil. According to them, man spontaneously knows that injustice or falsehood is bad and that it is obligatory to return what has been entrusted to one, to keep harm away from oneself, to show gratitude to one's benefactors, of whom God is the first. But the Ash'arites, who dominate Sunni orthodoxy, have upheld an opposing theory. As partisans of occasionalism, which does not recognize any consistency in nature, they consider that the divine positive revelation of God alone defines good and evil, right and wrong. Among the prescriptions of this divine positive law, many take up again or repeat the great elements of the moral patrimony of humanity and can be placed in relation to the Decalogue[13].

---

[13] *Koran*, sura 17, 22-38 (pp. 343-345): "Your Lord has decreed that you may adore none but Him. He has prescribed kindness with respect to your father and mother. If one of them or even both of them have attained old age near you, don't say to them: 'Fie'! do not push them away, but address them with respectful words. Take them kindly under your wing and say: 'My Lord! Be merciful towards them, as they were towards me at the time they raised me when I was an infant.' Your Lord knows perfectly what is in you. If you are just, he then is the one who pardons those who come back repentant to him. Give to your near of kin what is their due as well as to the poor and the traveler, but do not be wasteful. The wasteful are brothers of demons, and the Devil is very ungrateful towards his Lord. If, being in search of mercy that you hope from your Lord, you are obliged to go away, speak a benevolent word to them. Do not hold your hand closed at your neck, and neither extend it too generously; otherwise you would find yourself held in contempt and miserable. Yes, your Lord gives his gifts generously or sparingly to whom he wishes. He knows his servants quite well and he sees them perfectly. Do not kill your children for fear of poverty. He will provide for their subsistence along with your own. To kill them would be an enormous sin. Avoid fornication: it is an abomination! What a detestable path! Do not kill the man whom God has forbidden you to kill, except for a just reason. [...]. Do not touch the fortune of the orphan until he has come of age, except for its better use. Fulfill your commitments, for men will be interrogated on their commitments. Give a just measure when you measure; weigh with the most exact balance. This is something good and the result is excellent. Do not follow that of which you have no knowledge. There will surely be an accounting for all things: whatever is heard, seen or in the heart. Do not walk the earth with insolence. You cannot rip the earth apart or attain the height of mountains. What is evil in all this is detestable before the Lord".

1.2. The Greco-Roman sources of the natural law

18. The idea that there exists a norm of natural justice* prior to positive juridical determinations is already encountered in classical Greek culture with the exemplary figure of Antigone, the daughter of Oedipus. Her two brothers, Eteocles and Polyneices, confront each other to attain power and kill each other. Polyneices, the rebel, is condemned to remain unburied and burned on the pyre. But in order to fulfill the demands of piety towards her dead brother, Antigone appeals to "the unwritten and immutable laws" against the prohibition of burial pronounced by the king Creon.

"*Creon*: And so, you have dared to transgress my laws?
Antigone: Yes, for it was not Zeus who proclaimed them,
Nor justice which abides with the gods below
Neither the one nor the other established these laws among men;
I do not consider your decrees so powerful
That you, mortal man, can disregard the unwritten and immutable laws
of the gods.
They don't exist since today or yesterday but always;
No one knows when they appeared.
Out of fear of the wishes of a man
I ought not have risked being punished by the gods"[14].

19. Plato and Aristotle take up the distinction made by the Sophists between the laws that have their origin in a convention, that is, in a purely positive decision (*thesis*), and those that have force "by nature". The first are neither eternal nor are they in force everywhere and they do not oblige everyone. The second oblige everyone, always and everywhere[15]. Certain Sophists, like Callicles of Plato's *Gorgias*, had recourse to this distinction

---

* The term "droit natural" translated as "norm of natural justice."
[14] Sophocles, *Antigone*, v. 449-460.
[15] Cf. Aristotle, *Rhetoric*, I, XIII, 2 (1373 b 4-11): "Particular law is that which each group of men determines in relation to its members and these sorts of laws are divided into unwritten law and written law. Common law *(nomos koinos)* is that which is according to nature *(kata physin)*. In fact there is, as everyone recognizes by a kind of divination, a just and an unjust, common to all by nature, even though there is no communication or mutual covenant among peoples. Thus, one sees the Antigone of Sophocles declare that it is just to bury Polyneices, whose burial was forbidden, affirming that this burial is just, as being in accord with nature". Cf. also *Nichomachean Ethics* V, ch. 10.

in order to challenge the legitimacy of the laws instituted by human cities. To these laws, they opposed their narrow and erroneous idea of nature, reduced to its physical component alone. Thus, in opposition to the political and juridical equality of the citizens of the city, they advocated what seemed to them the most evident of the "natural laws": the stronger must prevail over the weaker[16].

20. There is nothing of this sort in Plato and Aristotle. They do not set the norm of natural justice in opposition to the positive laws of the city [πόλις]. They are convinced that the laws of the city are generally good and constitute the implementation, more or less successful, of a norm of natural justice which is in conformity with the nature of things. For Plato, the norm of natural justice is an ideal norm, a rule for both legislators and citizens, which permits the grounding and the evaluation of positive laws[17]. For Aristotle, this supreme norm of morality corresponds to the realization of the essential form of nature. What is natural is moral. The norm of natural justice is invariable; positive law changes according

---

[16] Cf. Plato, *Gorgias* (483c – 484b) [Speech of Callicles]: "Nature herself shows that it is just for the best to have more than the weakest, and the most powerful than the most helpless. She shows in many circumstances, that it works out well this way, as much in other living beings as in all the cities and races of men, and that the just is thus determined, by the fact that the most powerful commands the weakest and possesses a greater share. For on what conception of justice did Xerxes base his campaign against Greece, or his father against the Scythians? And one could cite innumerable other examples. But, it seems to me that these men did what they did according to the nature of the just and by Zeus, according to the law of nature, and, thus, probably not according to what was instituted by us, shaping the best and strongest among us, taking them from their youngest age, as one would do with lions, bewitching them with our spells and incantations, we enslave them by repeating that each one is equal to the others, and that this is the beautiful and the just. But if a man were born, endowed with a sufficiently strong nature, then, getting rid of all hindrances with a jolt, reducing them to pieces and fleeing them, stomping on our writings, our spells, our incantations and our laws, all without exception against and raising himself above us, behold, the slave thus reveals himself as our master, and then the just according to nature shines forth in full light".

[17] In the *Theaetetus* (172 a-b) Plato's Socrates displays the harmful political consequences of the relativistic thesis attributed to Protagoras according to which each man is the measure of truth: "Therefore, in politics, also, beautiful and ugly, just and unjust, pious and impious, all that each city believes as such and declares legally such for itself, all of this, in truth, is such for each one [...] In questions of just and unjust, of piety and impiety, one agrees to sustain rigorously that nothing of this is from nature and nothing possesses its essence exclusively; but simply what seems true to the group becomes true from the moment it seems such and for as long as it seems so".

to peoples and different epochs. But the norm of natural justice is not situated beyond positive law. It is embodied in the positive law, which is the application of the general idea of justice to social life in its variety.

21. In Stoicism, the natural law becomes the key concept of a universalist ethic. What is good and ought to be done is that which corresponds to nature, understood in both a physico-biological and rational sense. Every man, whatever the nation to which he belongs, must integrate himself as a part in the Whole of the universe. He must live according to his nature[18]. This imperative presupposes that an eternal law exists, a divine *Logos*, which is present both in the cosmos – which it infuses with rationality – as well as in human reason. Thus, for Cicero the law is the "the supreme reason inserted in nature, which commands what must be done and forbids the contrary"[19]. Nature and reason constitute the two sources of our knowledge of the fundamental ethical law, which is of divine origin.

1.3. The teaching of Sacred Scripture

22. The gift of the law on Sinai, of which the "Ten Words" constitute the centre, is an essential element of the religious experience of Israel. This law of the Covenant includes fundamental ethical precepts. They define the manner in which the chosen people must respond to God's choice by their holiness of life: "Say to all the congregation of the sons of Israel, you shall be holy; for I the Lord your God am holy" (*Lev* 19:2). But these ethical behaviours are also valid for other peoples, in that God demands an account from foreign nations that violate justice and what is right[20]. In fact, God had already sealed, in the person of Noah, a covenant with the totality of the human race, which implied, in particular, respect for life (*Gen* 9)[21]. More fundamentally, creation itself appears as the act by which

---

[18] Cf. for example, Seneca, *De vita beata*, VIII, 1: "It is nature that one must take as one's guide; it is nature that reason observes, and what it consults. To live happily or according to nature is, therefore, the same *(natura enim duce utendum est: hanc ratio observat, hanc consulit. Idem ergo beate vivere et secundum naturam)*".

[19] Cicero, *De legibus*, I, VI, 18: "Lex est ratio summa insita in natura quae iubet ea quae facienda sunt prohibetque contraria".

[20] Cf. *Amos* 1-2.

[21] Rabbinic Judaism refers to the seven moral imperatives that God gave to Noah for all men. They are enumerated in the Talmud (*Sanhedrin* 56): 1) You shall not commit idolatry; 2) You shall not kill; 3) You shall not steal; 4) You shall not commit adultery; 5) You shall not

God structures the entire universe by giving it a law: "Let them [the stars] praise the name of the Lord! For he commanded and they were created. And he has established them for ever and ever; he set down a law which cannot pass away" (*Ps* 148:5-6). This obedience of creatures to the law of God is a model for human beings.

23. Alongside the texts associated with the history of salvation, with the major theological themes of election, promise, law and covenant, the Bible also contains a wisdom literature that does not directly treat the national history of Israel, but deals with the place of man in the world. It develops the conviction that there is correct way, a "wise" way, of doing things and conducting one's life. Man must apply himself to the search for this wisdom and then make every effort to put it into practice. This wisdom is not so much found in history as in nature and everyday life[22]. In this literature, Wisdom is often presented as a divine perfection, sometimes hypostasized. In a striking way, she manifests herself in creation, of which she is "the fashioner" (*Wis* 7:22). The harmony that reigns among creatures bears witness to wisdom. In many ways, man is made a participant in this wisdom that comes from God. This participation is a gift from God, that one must ask for in the prayer: "I prayed, and understanding was given to me; I called upon God, and the spirit of wisdom came to me" (*Wis* 7:7). This wisdom is again the fruit of obedience to the revealed law. In fact, the Torah is like the incarnation of

---

blaspheme; 6) You shall not eat the flesh of a living animal; 7) You shall establish tribunals of justice to enforce respect for the preceding six commandments. If the 613 *mitzot* of the written Torah and their interpretation in the oral Torah only concern the Jews, the laws of Noah are addressed to all human beings.

[22] Wisdom literature is interested in history especially insofar as it shows forth certain constants in relation to the way that leads man towards God. The sages do not underestimate the lessons of history and their value as divine revelation (cf. *Sir* 44-51), but they have a vivid awareness that the connections among events depend on a coherence that is not itself an historical event. In order to comprehend this identity at the heart of mutability and to act in a responsible manner according to it, wisdom searches for principles and structural laws rather than precise historical perspectives. In so doing, wisdom literature concentrates on protology, namely, on creation at the beginning along with what it implies. In fact, protology attempts to describe the coherence that is found behind historical events. It is an *a priori* condition that permits the ordering of all possible historical events. Wisdom literature tries, therefore, to highlight the value of the conditions that make everyday life possible. History describes these elements in a successive manner; wisdom goes beyond history towards an a-temporal description of what constitutes reality at the time of creation, "in the beginning", when human beings were created in the image of God.

Wisdom. "If you desire wisdom, keep the commandments, and the Lord will supply it for you. For the fear of the Lord is wisdom and instruction" (*Sir* 1:26-27). But wisdom is also the result of a wise observation of nature and human morals in order to discover their immanent intelligibility and their exemplary value[23].

24. In the fullness of time, Jesus Christ preached the coming of the Kingdom as a manifestation of the merciful love of God made present among human beings through his own person and calling for conversion and the free response of love on their part. This preaching is not without consequences for ethics, for the way in which the world and human relations are to be structured. In his moral teaching, presented in a succinct form in the Sermon on the Mount, Jesus takes up the golden rule: "So, whatever you wish that men would do to you, do so to them; for this is the law and the prophets" (*Mt* 7:12)[24]. This positive precept completes the negative formulation of the same rule in the Old Testament: "And what you hate, do not do to anyone" (*Tob* 4:15)[25].

25. At the beginning of the Letter to the Romans, the Apostle Paul, intending to show the universal need for the salvation brought by Christ, describes the religious and moral situation common to all of humanity. He affirms the possibility of a natural knowledge of God: "For what can be known about God is plain to them, because God has shown it to them. Ever since the creation of the world his invisible nature, namely, his eternal power and deity, has been clearly perceived in the things that have been made" (*Rom* 1:19-20)[26]. But this knowledge has been perverted

---

[23] Cf. *Prov* 6:6-9: "Go to the ant, O sluggard; consider her ways, and be wise. Without having any chief, officer or ruler, she prepares her food in summer, and gathers her sustenance in harvest. How long will you lie there, O sluggard? When will you arise from your sleep?"

[24] Cf. also *Lk* 6:31: "And as you wish that men would do to you, do so to them".

[25] Cf. St. Bonaventure, *Commentarius in Evangelium Lucae*, c. 6, n. 76 (*Opera omnia*, VII, ed. Quaraechi, p. 156): "In hoc mandato [*Lk* 6:31] est consummatio legis naturalis, cuius una pars negativa ponitur Tobiae quarto et implicatur hic: 'Quod ab alio oderis tibi fieri, vide ne tu aliquando alteri facias'"; (Pseudo-) Bonaventura, *Expositio in Psalterium, Ps* 57,2 (*Opera onmia*, 1X, ed. Vivès, p. 227); "Duo sunt mandata naturalia: unum prohibitivum, unde hoc 'Quod tibi non vis fieri, alteri ne feceris'; aliud affirmativum, unde in Evangelio 'Omnia quaecumque vultis ut faciant vobis homines, eadem facite illis'. Primum de malis removendis, secundum de bonis adipiscendis".

[26] Cf. Vatican Council I, Dogmatic Constitution *Dei Filius, c.* 2. Cf. also *Acts* 14:16-17:

into idolatry. Placing Jews and pagans on the same level, Paul affirms the existence of an unwritten law inscribed in their hearts[27]. It permits everyone to discern good and evil by himself: "When Gentiles who do not have the law do by nature what the law requires, they are a law unto themselves, even though they do not have the law. They show that what the law requires is written on their hearts, while their conscience also bears witness and their conflicting thoughts accuse or perhaps excuse them" (*Rom* 2:14-15). Nevertheless, knowledge of the law does not in itself suffice in order to lead a righteous life[28]. These texts of St. Paul have had a decisive influence on Christian reflection in regard to natural law.

1.4. The developments of the Christian tradition

26. For the Fathers of the Church, the *sequi naturam* and the *sequela Christi* are not in opposition to each other. On the contrary, the Fathers generally adopt the idea from Stoicism that nature and reason indicate what our moral duties are. To follow nature and reason is to follow the personal *Logos*, the Word of God. The doctrine of the natural law, in fact, supplies a basis for completing biblical morality. Moreover, it allows us to explain why the pagans, independently of biblical revelation, possess a positive moral conception. This is indicated to them by nature and corresponds to the teaching of revelation. "From God are the law of nature and the law of revelation which function as one"[29]. The Fathers of the Church, however, do not purely and simply adopt the Stoic doctrine. They modify and develop it. On the one hand, the anthropology of biblical inspiration, which sees man as the *imago Dei* – the full truth of which is manifested

---

"In past generations he allowed all the nations to walk in their own ways; yet he did not leave himself without witness, for he did good and gave you from heaven rains and fruitful seasons, satisfying your hearts with food and gladness".

[27] In Philo of Alexandria, one finds the idea according to which Abraham, without the written law, was already leading "by nature" a life in conformity with the law. Cf. Philo of Alexandria, *De Abrahamo*, § 275-276 (translation by C.D. Yonge, *The Works of Philo Judaeus,* vol. 2 [London: Bohn, 1854], p. 452): "Moses says: 'This man [Abraham] fulfilled the divine law and all the commandments of God' (*Gen* 26:5), not having been taught to do so by written books, but in accordance with the unwritten law of his nature, being anxious to obey all healthful and salutary impulses".

[28] Cf. *Rom* 7:22-23: "I delight in the law of God, in my inmost self, but I see in my members another law at war with the law of my mind and making me captive to the law of sin which dwells in my members".

[29] Clement of Alexandria, *Stromata,* I, c. 29, 182, 1 (*Sources chrétiennes*, 30, p.176).

in Christ – forbids reducing the human person to a simple element of the cosmos: called to communion with the living God, the person transcends the whole cosmos while integrating himself in it. On the other hand, the harmony of nature and reason no longer rests on an immanentist vision of a pantheistic cosmos but on the common reference to the transcendent wisdom of the Creator. To conduct oneself in conformity with reason amounts to following the orientations that Christ, as the divine *Logos*, has set down by virtue of the *logoi spermatikoi* in human reason. To act against reason is an offense against these orientations. Very significant is the definition of St. Augustine: "The eternal law is the divine reason or the will of God, ordering the conservation of the natural order and forbidding its disruption"[30]. More precisely, for St. Augustine, the norms of the righteous life and of justice are expressed in the Word of God, who then imprints them in the heart of man "as the seal of a ring passes to the wax, but without leaving the ring"[31]. Moreover, for the Church Fathers the natural law is henceforth understood in the framework of the history of salvation, which leads to distinguishing different states of nature (original nature, fallen nature, restored nature) in which the natural law is realized in different ways. This Patristic doctrine of the natural law is transmitted to the Middle Ages, along with the closely related concept of the "law

---

[30] St. Augustine, *Contra Faustum*, xxii, c. 27 (PL 42, col. 418): "Lex vero aeterna est, ratio divina vel voluntas Dei, ordinem naturalem conservari iubens, perturbari vetans". For example, St. Augustine condemns lying because it goes directly against the nature of language and its calling to be the sign of thought; cf. *Enchiridion*, VII, 22 (*Corpus christianorum*, series latina, 46, p. 62): "Speech has not been given to men mutually to deceive each other, but rather to bring their thoughts to the knowledge of others. To make use of speech to deceive and not for its normal end is, therefore, a sin (Et utique verba propterea sunt institua non per quae invicem se homines fallant sed per quae in alterius quisque notitiam cogitationes suas perferat. Verbis ergo uti ad fallaciam, non ad quod instituta sunt, peccatum est)".

[31] St. Augustine, *De trinitate*, XIV, xv, 21 (*Corpus christianorum*, series latina, 50A, p. 451): "Where are these rules written? Where does the man, even an unjust one, recognize what is just? Where does he see that he must have what he himself does not have? Where are these written, except in the book of this light that one calls the Truth? It is that every just law is written; from there it passes into the heart of the man who practices justice, not that it migrates into him but places its imprint there, as the seal of a ring passes into the wax without leaving the ring (Ubinam sunt istae regulae scriptae, ubi quid sit justum et iniustus agnoscit, ubi cernit habendum esse quod ipse non habet? Ubi ergo scriptae sunt, nisi in libro lucis illius quae veritas dicitur unde omnis lex iusta describitur et in cor hominis qui operatur iustitiam non migrando sed tamquam imprimendo transfertur, sicut imago ex anulo et in ceram transit et anulum non relinquit?)".

of nations (*ius gentium*)", according to which there exist, apart from Roman civil law (*ius civile*), universal principles of law, which regulate the relations among peoples and are obligatory for all[32].

27. In the Middle Ages the doctrine of natural law attains a certain maturity and assumes a "classical" form that constitutes the background of all further discussion. It is characterized by four traits. In the first place, in conformity with the nature of scholastic thought that seeks to gather the truth wherever it is found, it takes up prior reflections on natural law, pagan or Christian, and tries to propose a synthesis. Second, in conformity with the systematic nature of scholastic thought, it locates natural law in a general metaphysical and theological framework. Natural law is understood as the rational creature's participation in the eternal, divine law, thanks to which it enters in a free and conscious manner into the plans of Providence. It is not a closed and complete set of moral norms, but a source of constant guidance, present and operative in the different stages of the economy of salvation. Third, with the recognition of the consistency of nature, in part linked to the rediscovery of the thought of Aristotle, the scholastic doctrine of the natural law considers the ethical and political order as a rational order, a work of human intelligence. The scholastic notion of natural law defines an autonomous space for that order, distinct but not separated from the order of religious revelation[33].

---

[32] Cf. Gaius, *Institutes*, 1. 1 (Second century A.D.) (ed. Julien Reinach, *Collection des universités de France* [Paris, 1950], p. 1): "Quod vero naturalis ratio inter onmes homines constituit, id apud onmes populos peraeque custoditur vocaturque ius gentium, quasi quo iure omnes gentes utuntur. Populus itaque romanus partim suo proprio, partim communi omnium hominum iure utitur".

[33] St. Thomas Aquinas clearly distinguishes the natural political order founded on reason and the supernatural religious order founded on the grace of revelation. He opposes the medieval Muslim and Jewish philosophers who attributed an essentially political role to religious revelation. Cf. *Quaestiones disputatae de veritate*, q. 12, a. 3, ad 11: "The society of men insofar as it is ordered to the end which is eternal life can only be conserved by the justice of the faith, whose principle is prophecy [...] But since this end is supernatural, both the justice ordered toward this end, and prophecy, which is its principle, will be supernatural. In truth, the justice by which human society is governed and ordered towards the good of the city, can be sufficiently achieved by means of the principles of the *ius naturale* implanted in men". (Societas hominum secundum quod ordinatur ad finem vitae aeternae, non potest conservari nisi per iustitiam fidei, cuius principium est prophetia [...] Sed cum hic finis sit supernaturalis, et iustitia ad hunc finem ordinata, et prophetia, quae est eius principium, erit supernaturalis. Iustitia vero per quam gubernatur societas humana in ordine ad bonum civile, sufficienter potest haberi per principia iuris naturalis homini indita)".

Finally, in the eyes of scholastic theologians and jurists, natural law constitutes a point of reference and a criterion in the light of which they evaluate the legitimacy of positive laws and of particular customs.

1.5. Further developments

28. In certain aspects, the modern history of the idea of natural law represents a legitimate development of the teaching of medieval scholasticism in a more complex cultural context, marked in particular by a more vivid sense of moral subjectivity. Among these developments, we point out the works of the Spanish theologians of the 16th century, who, following the example of the Dominican Francis of Vitoria, had recourse to natural law to contest the imperialist ideology of some Christian states of Europe and to defend the rights of the non-Christian peoples of America. In fact, such rights are inherent in human nature and do not depend on one's concrete situation vis-à-vis the Christian faith. The idea of natural law also allowed the Spanish theologians to establish the foundations of an international law, i.e., of a universal norm that regulates the relations of peoples and states among themselves.

29. But in other aspects the idea of natural law in the modern age took on orientations and forms that contributed to making it difficult to accept today. During the last centuries of the Middle Ages, there developed in scholasticism a current of voluntarism, the cultural hegemony of which has profoundly modified the idea of natural law. Voluntarism proposes to highlight the transcendence of the free subject in relation to all conditioning. Against naturalism that tended to subject God to the laws of nature, it emphasizes, in a unilateral way, the absolute freedom of God, with the risk of compromising his wisdom and rendering his decisions arbitrary. In the same manner, against intellectualism, suspected of subjecting the human person to the order of the world, it exalts a freedom of indifference, understood as a pure capacity to choose contraries, which runs the risk of disconnecting the person from his natural inclinations and from the objective good[34].

---

[34] Cf. BENEDICT XVI, *Discourse at Regensburg on the occasion of the meeting with the representatives of the world of science*. (September 12, 2006), in AAS 98 [2006] 733): "In the late Middle Ages we find trends in theology which would sunder this synthesis between the Greek spirit and the Christian spirit. In contrast with the so-called intellectualism of Augustine and Thomas, there arose with Duns Scotus a voluntarism which, in its later

30. The consequences of voluntarism for the doctrine of natural law are numerous. Above all, while in St. Thomas Aquinas the law was understood as a work of reason and an expression of wisdom, voluntarism leads one to connect the law to will alone, and to a will detached from its intrinsic ordering to the good. Henceforth, all the force of the law resides only in the will of the lawmaker. The law is thus divested of its intrinsic intelligibility. In these conditions, morality is reduced to obedience to the commandments that manifest the will of the lawmaker. Thomas Hobbes will end up holding the position that *auctoritas, non veritas, facit legem* (it is authority and not truth that makes law)[35]. Modern man, loving autonomy, could only rebel against such a vision of the law. Then, with the pretext of preserving the absolute sovereignty of God over nature, voluntarism deprives it of all internal intelligibility. The thesis of the *potentia Dei absoluta*, according to which God could act independently of his wisdom and his goodness, relativizes all the existing intelligible structures and weakens the natural knowledge that man can have of them. Nature ceases to be a criterion for knowing the wise will of God: man can expect this knowledge only from a revelation.

31. In addition, several factors have led to the secularization of the notion of natural law. Among these, one can recall the increasing divide between faith and reason which characterizes the end of the Middle Ages or some aspects of the Reformation[36], but above all the will to overcome the violent

---

developments, led to the claim that we can only know God's *voluntas ordinata*. Beyond this is the realm of God's freedom, in virtue of which he could have done the opposite of everything he has actually done. This gives rise to positions which [...] might even lead to the image of a capricious God, who is not even bound to truth and goodness. God's transcendence and otherness are so exalted that our reason, our sense of the true and good, are no longer an authentic mirror of God, whose deepest possibilities remain eternally unattainable and hidden behind his actual decisions".

[35] This phrase appears in the Latin version of Thomas Hobbes, *Leviathan* (see François Tricaud, *Léviathan* [Paris: Sirey, 1971], p. 295, note 81). The English text states: "The interpretation of the laws of nature in a commonwealth dependeth not on the books of moral philosophy. The authority of writers, without the authority of the commonwealth, maketh not their opinions law, be they never so true... it is by the sovereign power that it is law."

[36] The attitude of the Reformers with respect to the natural law was not monolithic. Basing himself on St. Paul, John Calvin – more than Martin Luther – recognized the existence of the natural law as an ethical norm even if it is radically incapable of justifying man. "It is a common thing, that man is sufficiently instructed in the correct rule of living well by this natural law of which the Apostle speaks [...]. The end of the natural law is to render man inexcusable; this, therefore, allows us to define it properly: it is an awareness of the

religious conflicts that bloodied Europe up until the dawn of modern times. Thus a desire arose to establish the political unity of human communities by putting religious confession in parentheses. Henceforth, the doctrine of natural law prescinds from all particular religious revelation, and therefore from all confessional theology. It claims to be founded solely on the light of reason common to all people and is presented as the ultimate norm in the secular field.

32. Further, modern rationalism posits the existence of an absolute and normative order of intelligible essences accessible to reason and accordingly relativizes the reference to God as the ultimate foundation of the natural law. Certainly, the necessary, eternal, and immutable order of essences needs to be actualized by the Creator, but it is believed that this order already possesses in itself its coherence and rationality. Reference to God therefore becomes optional. The natural law would be binding on all "even if there were no God (*etsi Deus non daretur*)"[37].

33. The modern rationalist model of natural law is characterized: 1) by the essentialist belief in an immutable and ahistorical human nature, of which reason can perfectly grasp the definition and essential properties; 2) by putting into parentheses the concrete situation of human persons in the history of salvation, marked by sin and grace, which however have a decisive influence on the knowledge and practice of the natural law; 3) by the idea that it is possible for reason to deduce *a priori* the precepts of the natural law, beginning from the definition of the essence of the human being; 4) by the maximal extension thus given to those deduced precepts, so that natural law appears as a code of pre-made laws regulating almost the entire range of behaviour. This tendency to extend the field of the determinations

---

conscience by which it discerns sufficiently between good and evil in order to remove man from the cover of ignorance, so that he is reproached by his very own testimony" (*Institutes of the Christian Religion*, book II, ch. 2, 22). During the three centuries that follow the Reformation, the natural law served as a foundation for jurisprudence among Protestants. Only with the secularization of the natural law did Protestant theology, in the 19th century, distance itself from it. Only then does an opposition between Protestant and Catholic opinions on the natural law becomes apparent. In our own time, however, Protestant ethics seems to be showing renewed interest in this notion [of the natural law].

[37] This expression finds its origin in Hugo Grotius, *De jure belli et pacis*, Prolegomena: "Haec quidem quae iam diximus locum aliquem haberent, etsi daremus, quod sine summo scelere dari nequit, non esse Deum".

of natural law was at the origin of a grave crisis when, particularly with the rapid development of the human sciences, Western thought became more aware of the historicity of human institutions and of the cultural relativity of many ways of acting that at times had been justified by appeal to the evidence of natural law. The gap between an abstract maximalist theory and the complexity of the empirical data explains in part the disaffection for the very idea of natural law. In order that the notion of natural law can be of use in the elaboration of a universal ethic in a secularized and pluralistic society such as our own, it is therefore necessary to avoid presenting it in the rigid form that it assumed, particularly in modern rationalism.

1.6. The Magisterium of the Church and natural law

34. Before the 13th century, because the distinction between the natural and the supernatural order was not clearly elaborated, natural law was generally assimilated into Christian morals. Thus the decree of Gratian, which provides the fundamental canonical norm in the 12th century, begins thus: "Natural law is that which is contained in the law and in the Gospel". It then identifies the content of the natural law with the golden rule and explains that the divine laws correspond to nature[38]. The Fathers of the Church had recourse to natural law and to Sacred Scripture to provide a foundation for the moral behaviour of Christians, but the Magisterium of the Church, early on, had to make very few interventions to settle disputes on the content of the moral law.

When the Magisterium of the Church was led not only to resolve particular moral discussions, but also to justify its own position before a secularized world, it appealed more explicitly to the notion of natural law. It is in the 19th century, especially during the pontificate of Leo XIII, that recourse to natural law becomes more necessary in the acts of the Magisterium. The most explicit presentation is found in the Encyclical *Libertas praestantissimum* (1888). Leo XIII refers to natural law to identify the source of civil authority and to fix its limits. He vigorously recalls that one must obey God rather than men when the civil authorities command or

---

[38] Gratian, *Concordantia discordantium canonum*, pars 1, dist. 1 (PL 187, col. 29): "Humanum genus duobus regitur, naturali videlicet iure et moribus. Ius naturale est quod in lege et Evangelio continetur, quo quisque iubetur alii facere quod sibi vult fieri, et prohibetur alii inferre quod sibi nolit fieri. [...] Omnes leges aut divinae sunt aut humanae. Divinae natura, humanae moribus constant, ideoque hae discrepant, quoniam aliae aliis gentibus placent".

recognize something contrary to divine law or to the natural law. He also looks to natural law to protect private property against socialism and to defend the right of workers to an adequate living wage. In this same line, John XXIII refers to natural law to provide a foundation for the rights and the duties of man (Encyclical *Pacem in terris* [1963]). With Pius XI (Encyclical *Casti connubii* [1930]) and Paul VI (Encyclical *Humanae vitae* [1968]), natural law is revealed as a decisive criterion for questions relating to conjugal morality. Certainly, natural law is a law accessible to human reason, common to believers and nonbelievers, and the Church does not have exclusive rights over it, but since revelation assumes the requirements of the natural law, the Magisterium of the Church has been established as the guarantor and interpreter of it[39]. The *Catechism of the Catholic Church* (1992) and the Encyclical *Veritatis splendor* (1993) assign a decisive place to the natural law in the exposition of Christian morals[40].

35. Today the Catholic Church invokes the natural law in four principal contexts. In the first place, facing the spread of a culture that limits rationality to the positive sciences and abandons the moral life to relativism, it insists on the natural capacity of human beings to obtain by reason "the ethical message contained in being[41]" and to know in their main lines the fundamental norms of just action in conformity with their nature and their dignity. The natural law thus responds to the need to provide a basis in reason for the rights of man[42] and makes possible an intercultural and interreligious dialogue capable of fostering universal peace and of avoiding the "clash of civilizations". In the second place, in the presence of relativistic individualism, which judges that every

---

[39] Cf. PAUL VI, Encyclical *Humanae vitae*, n. 4 (AAS 60 [1968], p. 483).

[40] Cf. *Catechism of the Catholic Church*, n. 1954-1960; JOHN PAUL II, Encyclical *Veritatis splendor*, n. 40-53.

[41] BENEDICT XVI, *Speech of February 12, 2007 to the International Congress on Natural Moral Law organized by the Pontifical Lateran University* (AAS 99 [2007], p. 243).

[42] Cf. BENEDICT XVI, *Address of April 18, 2008 before the General Assembly of the United Nations:* "These rights [the rights of man] are based on the natural law inscribed on the heart of man and present in the different cultures and civilizations. To detach human rights from this context would mean restricting their range and yielding to a relativistic conception, according to which the meaning and interpretation of rights could vary and their universality could be denied in the name of different cultural, political, and social conceptions and even religious outlooks".

individual is the source of his own values, and that society results from a mere contract agreed upon by individuals who choose to establish all the norms themselves, it recalls the non-conventional, but natural and objective character of the fundamental norms that regulate social and political life. In particular, the democratic form of government is intrinsically bound to stable ethical values, which have their source in the requirements of natural law and thus do not depend on the fluctuations of the consent of a numerical majority. In the third place, facing an aggressive secularism that wants to exclude believers from public debate, the Church points out that the interventions of Christians in public life on subjects that regard natural law (the defence of the rights of the oppressed, justice in international relations, the defence of life and of the family, religious freedom and freedom of education), are not in themselves of a confessional nature, but derive from the care which every citizen must have for the common good of society. In the fourth place, facing the threats of the abuse of power, and even of totalitarianism, which juridical positivism conceals and which certain ideologies propagate, the Church recalls that civil laws do not bind in conscience when they contradict natural law, and asks for the acknowledgment of the right to conscientious objection, as well as the duty of disobedience in the name of obedience to a higher law[43]. The reference to natural law, far from producing conformism, guarantees personal freedom and defends the marginalized and those oppressed by social structures which do not take the common good into account.

---

[43] Cf. John Paul II, Encyclical *Evangelium vitae*, n. 73-74.

CHAPTER 2: THE PERCEPTION OF COMMON MORAL VALUES

36. The examination of the great traditions of moral wisdom undertaken in the first chapter shows that certain kinds of human behaviour are recognized, in the majority of cultures, as expressing a certain excellence in the way in which a human being lives and realizes his own humanity: acts of courage, patience in the trials and difficulties of life, compassion for the weak, moderation in the use of material goods, a responsible attitude in relation to the environment, and dedication to the common good. Such ethical conduct defines the main lines of a properly moral ideal of a life "according to nature", that is, in conformity with the profound being of the human subject. On the other hand, some forms of behaviour are universally recognized as calling for condemnation: murder, theft, lying, wrath, greed, and avarice. These appear as attacks on the dignity of the human person and on the just requirements of life in society. One is justified to see in this consensus a manifestation of that which – beyond the diversity of cultures – is the human in the human being, namely "human nature". But at the same time, one must admit that such agreement on the moral quality of certain behaviour coexists with a great variety of explanatory theories. Whether we look at the fundamental doctrines of the Upanishads in Hinduism, or the four "noble truths" of Buddhism, or the Tao of Lao-Tse, or the "nature" of the Stoics, every school of wisdom or every philosophical system understands moral action within a general explanatory framework that comes to legitimize the distinction between what is good and what is evil. There is a diversity among these explanations, which makes both dialogue and the grounding of moral norms difficult.

37. Nevertheless, apart from any theoretical justifications of the concept of natural law, it is possible to illustrate the immediate data of the conscience of which it wants to give an account. The object of the present chapter is precisely to show how the common moral values that constitute natural law are grasped. It is only later that we will see how the concept of natural law rests on an explanatory framework which both undergirds and legitimizes moral values, in a way that can be shared by many. To do this, the presentation of the natural law by St. Thomas Aquinas appears

particularly pertinent, since, among other things, it places the natural law within a morality that sustains the dignity of the human person and recognizes his capacity of discernment[44].

2.1. The role of society and culture

38. The human person only progressively comes to moral experience and becomes capable of expressing to himself the precepts that should guide his action. The person attains this to degree to which he is inserted in a network of human relationships from birth, beginning with the family, relationships which allow him, little by little, to become aware of himself and of reality around him. This is done in particular by the learning of a language – one's mother tongue – which teaches the person to name things and allows him to become a subject aware of himself. Oriented by the persons who surround him, permeated by the culture in which he is immersed, the person recognizes certain ways of behaving and of thinking as values to pursue, laws to observe, examples to imitate, visions of the world to accept. The social and cultural context thus exercises a decisive role in the education in moral values. There is, however, no contradiction between such conditioning and human freedom. Rather, it makes freedom possible, since it is through such conditioning that the person is able to come to moral experience, which will eventually allow him to review some of the "obvious facts" that he had interiorized in the course of his moral apprenticeship. Moreover, in the present context of globalization, societies and cultures themselves must inevitably practice sincere dialogue and exchange, based on the co-responsibility of all in regard to the common good of the planet: they must leave aside particular interests to attain the moral values that all are called to share.

2.2. Moral experience: "one must do good"

39. Every human being who attains self-awareness and responsibility experiences an interior call to do good. He discovers that he is fundamentally a moral being, capable of perceiving and of expressing the call that, as we have seen, is found within all cultures: "One must do good and avoid evil". All the other precepts of the natural law are based

---

[44] Cf. JOHN PAUL II., Encyclical *Veritatis splendor*, n. 44: "The Church has often made reference to the Thomistic doctrine of natural law, including it in her own teaching on morality".

on this precept[45]. This first precept is known naturally, immediately, by the practical reason, just as the principle of non-contradiction (the intellect cannot at the same time and under the same aspect both affirm and deny the same thing about something) which is at the base of all speculative reasoning, is grasped intuitively, naturally, by the theoretical reason, when the subject comprehends the sense of the terms employed. Traditionally, such knowledge of the first principle of the moral life is attributed to an innate intellectual disposition called *synderesis*[46].

40. With this principle, we find ourselves immediately in the sphere of morality. The good that thus imposes itself on the person is in fact the moral good; it is behaviour that, going beyond the categories of what is useful, is in keeping with the authentic realization of this being – at the same time one and differentiated – who is the human person. Human activity cannot be reduced to a simple question of adaptation to the "ecosystem": to be human is to exist and to be placed within a broader framework that defines meaning, values and responsibilities. By searching for the moral good, the person contributes to the realization of his nature, beyond impulses of instinct or the search for a particular pleasure. This moral good testifies to itself and is understood from itself[47].

41. The moral good corresponds to the profound desire of the human person who — like every being — tends spontaneously, naturally, towards realizing himself fully, towards that which allows him to attain the perfection proper to him, namely, happiness. Unfortunately, the subject can always allow himself to be drawn by particular desires and

---

[45] St. Thomas Aquinas, *Summa theologiae*, I-II, q. 94, a. 2: "The first precept of the law is that the good is to be done and pursued and evil is to be avoided. And upon this precept all the other precepts of the law of nature are based: namely that all those things to be done or avoided pertain to the precepts of the law of nature, which practical reason naturally apprehends to be human goods (Hoc est […] primum praeceptum legis, quod bonum est faciendum et prosequendum, et malum vitandum. Et super hoc fundantur omnia alia legis naturae, ut scililicet omnia illa facienda vel vitanda pertineant ad praecepta legis naturae, quae ratio practica naturaliter apprehendit esse bona humana)".

[46] Cf. St. Thomas Aquinas, *Summa theologiae*, I, q. 79, a. 12: *Catechism of the Catholic Church*, n. 1780

[47] Cf. Romano Guardini, Freedom, Grace, and Destiny: *Three Chapters on the Interpretation of Existence* (translation by John Murray, S.J., [New York: Pantheon, 1961, p. 48): "Good action also signifies action that fructifies and enriches being. Good preserves life and completes it, but only when it is done for its own sake".

to choose goods or to do deeds that go against the moral good which he perceives. A person can refuse to go beyond himself. It is the price of a freedom limited in itself and weakened by sin, a freedom that encounters only particular goods, none of which can fully satisfy the human heart. It pertains to the reason of the subject to examine if these particular goods can be integrated into the authentic realization of the person: if so, they will be judged morally good, and if not, morally bad.

42. This last claim is of capital importance. It is the basis of the possibility of dialogue with persons belonging to different cultural or religious horizons. It values the eminent dignity of every human person, in stressing his natural aptitude to know the moral good that he must accomplish. Like every creature, the human person is defined by a combination of dynamisms and finalities, prior to the free choices of the will. But, unlike beings that are not endowed with reason, the human person is capable of knowing and of interiorizing these finalities, and thus of appreciating, in accordance with them that which is good or bad for him. Thus he recognizes the eternal law, i.e., the plan of God regarding creation, and participates in God's providence in a particularly excellent manner, guiding himself and guiding others[48]. This insistence on the dignity of the moral subject and on his relative autonomy is rooted in the recognition of the autonomy of created realities and corresponds to a fundamental given of contemporary culture[49].

---

[48] Cf. St. THOMAS AQUINAS, *Summa theologiae, Ia-IIae,* q. 91, a. 2: "But among all others, the rational creature is subject to divine providence in a more excellent way than all beings, insofar as it partakes of a share of providence, providing both for itself and for others. Thus it has a share of the Eternal Reason, whereby it has a natural inclination to its proper act and end. This participation of the eternal law in the rational creature is called natural law. (Inter cetera autem rationalis creatura excellentiori quodam modo divinae providentiae subiacet, inquantum et ipsa fit providentiae particeps, sibi ipsi et aliis providens. Unde et in ipsa participatur ratio aeterna, per quarn habet naturalem inclinationem ad debitum actum et finem. Et talis participatio legis aetemae in rationali creatura lex naturalis dicitur)". This text is cited in JOHN PAUL II, Encyclical *Veritatis splendor,* n. 43. Cf. also VATICAN COUNCIL II, Declaration *Dignitatis humanae,* n. 3: "The highest norm of human life is the divine law – eternal, objective and universal – whereby God orders, directs and governs the entire universe and all the ways of the human community, by a plan conceived in wisdom and love. Man has been made by God to participate in this law, with the result that, under the gentle disposition of divine Providence, he can come to perceive ever increasingly the unchanging truth".

[49] VATICAN COUNCIL II, Pastoral Constitution *Gaudium et spes,* n. 36.

43. The moral obligation that the subject recognizes does not come, therefore, from a law that would be exterior to him (pure heteronomy), but arises from within the subject himself. In fact, as indicated by the maxim we have cited – "One must do good and avoid evil" – the moral good that reason determines "imposes itself" on the subject. It "ought" to be accomplished. It takes on a character of obligation and of law. But the term "law" here does not refer to scientific laws that limit themselves to describing the factual constants of the physical or social world, nor to an imperative imposed arbitrarily on the moral subject from without. Law here designates an orientation of the practical reason which indicates to the moral subject what kind of action is in accord with the basic and necessary dynamism of his being that tends to its full realization. This law is normative in virtue of an internal requirement of the spirit. It springs from the heart itself of our being as a call to the realization and transcending of oneself. It is not therefore a matter of subjecting oneself to the law of another, but of accepting the law of one's own being.

2.3. The discovery of the precepts of the natural law: universality of the natural law

44. Once we posit the basic affirmation that introduces us to the moral order – "One must do good and avoid evil" – we see how the recognition of the fundamental laws that ought to govern human action take effect in the subject. Such recognition is not the fact of an abstract consideration of human nature, nor of the effort of conceptualization, which will afterwards be the distinctive characteristic of philosophical and theological theorizing. The perception of fundamental moral goods is immediate, vital, based on the connaturality of the spirit with values, and engages affectivity as much as intelligence, the heart as much as the mind. It is an acquisition often imperfect, still obscure and dim, but it has the profundity of immediacy. It deals with the data of the most simple and common experience, implicit in the concrete action of persons.

45. In his search for the moral good, the human person sets himself to listen to what he is, and takes note of the fundamental inclinations of his nature, which are something quite different from the simple blind impulses of desire. Perceiving that the goods to which he tends by nature are necessary for his moral realization, he formulates for himself, under

the form of practical commands, the moral duty of actualizing them in his own life. He expresses to himself a certain number of very general precepts that he shares with all other human beings and that constitute the content of that which we call natural law.

46. One traditionally distinguishes three great sets of natural dynamisms that are at work in the human person[50]. The first, which is in common with all substances, comprises essentially the inclination to preserve and to develop one's own existence. The second, which is in common with all living things, comprises the inclination to reproduce, in order to perpetuate the species. The third, which is proper to the human person as a rational being, comprises the inclination to know the truth about God and to live in society. From these inclinations, the first precepts of the natural law, known naturally, can be formulated. Such precepts remain very general, but they form the first substratum that is at the foundation of all further reflections on the good to be practiced and on the evil to be avoided.

47. To leave this generality and to make clear the concrete choices about what to do, it is necessary to have recourse to discursive reason, which will determine what are the concrete moral goods capable of fulfilling the person – and humanity – and will formulate more concrete precepts capable of guiding him in his action. In this new stage the knowledge of the moral good proceeds by way of reasoning. At its origin this reasoning remains very simple: a limited experience of life suffices, and it remains within the intellectual possibility of everyone. One speaks here of the "secondary precepts" of the natural law, discovered through the consideration (to varying degrees) of practical reason, in contrast to the general fundamental precepts that reason picks up spontaneously and which are called "primary precepts"[51].

2.4. The precepts of the natural law

48. We have identified in the human person a first inclination that he shares with all beings: the inclination to preserve and develop his own existence. In living beings there is habitually a spontaneous reaction to an

---

[50] Cf. St. Thomas Aquinas, *Summa theologiae, Ia-IIae,* q. 94, a. 2.

[51] Cf. Ibid., *Ia-IIae,* q. 94, a. 6.

imminent danger of death: one flees it, one defends the integrity of one's own existence, one struggles to survive. Physical life appears naturally as the fundamental, essential, primordial good, from which comes the precept to protect one's own life. Within this category of the preservation of life are included the inclinations to everything that contributes, in a way proper to the human person, to the maintenance and quality of biological life: bodily integrity; the use of external goods necessary for the sustenance and the integrity of life, such as food, clothing, housing, work; the quality of the biological environment... Taking his bearings from these inclinations, the human being formulates for himself goals to be realized that contribute to the harmonious and responsible development of his own being and which, as such, appear to him as moral goods, values to pursue, duties to accomplish and indeed as rights to assert. In fact, the duty to preserve one's own life has as its correlative the right to demand that which is necessary for one's preservation in a favourable environment[52].

49. The second inclination, which is common to all living beings, concerns the survival of the species that is realized by procreation. Reproduction is included in the prolongation of the tendency to persevere in being. If the perpetuity of biological existence is impossible for the individual himself, it is possible for the species and, thus, in a certain measure, overcomes the limits inherent in every physical being. The good of the species appears in this way as one of the fundamental aspirations present in the person. We become particularly aware of it in our time, when certain issues such as global warming revive our sense of responsibility for the planet, as well as for the human species in particular. This openness to a certain common good of the species is already an assertion of certain aspirations proper to the human person. The dynamism towards procreation is intrinsically linked to the natural inclination that leads man to woman and woman to man, a universal datum recognized in all societies. It is the same for the inclination to care for one's children and to educate them. These inclinations imply that the permanence of the union of man and woman, indeed even their mutual fidelity, are already values to pursue, even if they can only fully flourish in the spiritual order of interpersonal communion[53].

---

[52] Cf. *Universal Declaration of Human Rights,* articles. 3,5,17,22.
[53] Cf. Ibid., article 16.

50. The third set of inclinations is specific to the human being as a spiritual being, endowed with reason, capable of knowing the truth, of entering into dialogue with others and of forming relations of friendship. Therefore, this third level is particularly important. The inclination to live in society derives first of all from the fact that the human being has need of others to overcome his own intrinsic individual limits and to achieve maturity in the various spheres of his existence. But for his spiritual nature to fully flourish, a person has the need to form relations of generous friendship with his fellow human beings and to develop intense cooperation in the search for the truth. His integral good is so intimately linked to life in community that he enters into political society by virtue of a natural inclination and not by mere convention[54]. The relational character of the person also expresses itself by the tendency to live in communion with God or the absolute. It manifests itself in religious sentiment and in the desire to know God. Certainly, it can be denied by those who refuse to admit the existence of a personal God, but it remains implicitly present in the search for truth and meaning, experienced by every human being.

51. Corresponding to these tendencies that are specific to the human person, there is the need, recognized by reason, to realize concretely this life in relationship and to construct life in society on just foundations that correspond to the norm of natural justice. This entails the recognition of the equal dignity of every individual of the human species, beyond the differences of race and culture, and a great respect for humanity wherever it is found, including that of the smallest and in the most despised of its members. "Do not do to another that which you would not want done to you". Here we encounter the golden rule, which today is posited as the very principle of a morality of reciprocity. In the first chapter of this text, we were able to find the presence of this rule in the greater parts of the wisdom traditions, as well as in the Gospel itself. It is in referring to a negative formulation of the golden rule that St. Jerome manifested the universality of several moral precepts. "That is why the judgment of God is just, who writes in the heart of the human race: 'That which you do not want done to you, do not do to another'. Who does not know that homicide, adultery, theft and every kind of greed are evil, since one does

---

[54] Cf. Aristotle, *Politics*, I, 2 (1253 a 2-3); Vatican Council II, Pastoral Constitution *Gaudium et spes*, n. 12, § 4.

not want them done to oneself? If a person did not know that these things were bad, he would never complain when they are inflicted on him"[55]. To the golden rule are linked several commandments of the Decalogue, as are numerous Buddhist precepts, and, indeed, some Confucian rules, and also the greater part of the orientations of the great Charters that enumerate the rights of the person.

52. After this brief exposition of the moral principles that derive from reason's consideration of the fundamental inclinations of the human person, we find a set of precepts and values that, at least in their general formulation, can be considered as universal, since they apply to all humanity. They also take on the character of immutability to the extent that they derive from a human nature whose essential components remain the same throughout history. It can still happen that they are obscured or even erased from the human heart because of sin and because of cultural and historical conditioning, which can negatively affect the personal moral life: ideologies and insidious propaganda, generalized relativism, structures of sin[56]. We must therefore be modest and prudent when invoking the "obviousness" of natural law precepts. But this does not mean that we cannot recognize in these precepts the common foundation for a dialogue in search of a universal ethic. Those undertaking such a dialogue, however, must learn to distance themselves from their own particular interests, in order to be open to the needs of others, and to allow themselves to be summoned by the common moral values. In a pluralistic society, where it is difficult to agree on philosophical foundations, such a dialogue is absolutely necessary. The doctrine of natural law can make its contribution to such a dialogue.

---

[55] St. Jerome, *Epistola* 121, 8 (PL 22, col. 1025).

[56] Cf. St. Thomas Aquinas, *Summa theologiae*, Ia-IIae, q. 94, a. 6: "But as regards the other secondary precepts, the natural law can be destroyed from men's hearts, either on account of evil persuasions—just as also in speculative matters errors may arise concerning necessary conclusions—or on account of depraved customs and corrupt habits, as some men did not consider stealing a sin, or even the vices against nature, as the Apostle says in Rom 1:24). (Quantum vero ad alia praecepta secundaria, potest lex naturalis deleri de cordibus hominum, vel propter malas persuasiones, eo modo quo etiam in speculativis errores contingunt circa conclusiones necessarias; vel etiam propter pravas consuetudines et habitus corruptos; sicut apud quosdam non reputabantur latrocinia peccata, vel etiam vitia contra naturam, ut etiam apostolus dicit, ad Rom 1)".

2.5. The application of the common precepts: historicity of the natural law

53. It is impossible to remain at the level of generality, which is that of the first principles of the natural law. In fact, moral reflection must descend into the concreteness of action to throw its light on it. But the more it faces concrete and contingent situations, the more its conclusions are affected by a note of variability and uncertainty. It is not surprising, therefore, that the concrete application of the precepts of the natural law can take different forms in different cultures, or even in different epochs within a single culture. It is sufficient to recall the evolution of moral reflection on questions such as slavery, lending at interest, duelling or the death penalty. Sometimes such evolution leads to a better comprehension of moral requirements. Sometimes, in addition, the evolution of the political or economic situation leads to a re-evaluation of particular norms that had been established before. Morality, in fact, deals with contingent realities that evolve over time. Although he lived in the epoch of Christendom, a theologian such as St. Thomas Aquinas had a very clear perception of this. Practical reason, he wrote in the *Summa theologiae*, "deals with contingent realities, about which human actions are concerned. Therefore, although there is some necessity in the general principles, the more we descend to particular matters, the more we encounter indeterminacy... In matters of action, truth or practical rectitude is not the same for all in its particular applications, but only in its general principles: and where there is the same rectitude in particular actions, it is not equally known to all. ... And here, the more one descends to particulars the more the indeterminacy grows"[57].

54. This perspective gives an account of the historicity of natural law, whose concrete applications can vary over time. At the same time, it opens the door to the reflection of moralists, inviting them to dialogue and to discussion. This is all the more necessary because in morality pure

---

[57] ST. THOMAS AQUINAS, *Summa theologiae, Ia-IIae*, q. 94, a. 4: (Ratio practica negotiatur circa contingentia, in quibus sunt operationes humanae, et ideo, etsi in communibus sit aliqua necessitas, quanto magis ad propria descenditur, tanto magis invenitur defectus [...] In operativis autem non est eadem veritas vel rectitudo practica apud omnes quantum al propria, sed solum quantum ad communia, et apud illos apud quod est eadem rectitudo in propriis, non est aequaliter omnibus nota. [...] Et hoc tanto magis invenitur deficere, quanto magis ad particularia descenditur)".

deduction by syllogism is not adequate. The more the moralist confronts concrete situations, the more he must have recourse to the wisdom of experience, an experience that integrates the contributions of the other sciences and is nourished by contact with men and women engaged in the action. Only this wisdom of experience enables one to consider the multiplicity of circumstances and to arrive at a position on how to accomplish what is good *hic et nunc*. The moralist must also (and this is the difficulty of his work) have recourse to the combined resources of theology, of philosophy, as well as of the human, economic and biological sciences, in order to discern clearly the given facts of the situation and to identify correctly the concrete requirements of human dignity. At the same time, he must be particularly attentive to safeguard the fundamental givens expressed by the precepts of the natural law that remain valid despite cultural variations.

2.6. The moral dispositions of the person and his concrete action

55. To reach a just evaluation of the things to be done, the moral subject must be endowed with a certain number of interior dispositions that allow him both to be open to the demands of the natural law and, at the same time, informed about the givens of the concrete situation. In the context of pluralism, which is ours, one is more and more aware that one cannot elaborate a morality based on the natural law without including a reflection on the interior dispositions or virtues that render the moralist capable of elaborating an adequate norm of action. This is even more true for the subject personally engaged in action and who must formulate a judgment of conscience. It is, therefore, not surprising that one witnesses today a new blossoming of "virtue ethics" inspired by the Aristotelian tradition. Insisting in this way on the moral qualities required for adequate moral reflection, one comprehends the important role that the various cultures attribute to the figure of the wise man. He enjoys a particular capacity of discernment in the measure in which he possesses the interior moral dispositions that allow him to formulate an adequate ethical judgment. A discernment of this kind should characterize both the moralist, when he endeavours to concretize the precepts of the natural law, as well as every autonomous subject charged with making a judgment of conscience and with formulating the immediate and concrete norm for his action.

56. Morality cannot, therefore, be content with producing norms. It should also favour the formation of the subject so that, engaged in action, he may be capable of adapting the universal precepts of the natural law to the concrete conditions of existence in diverse cultural contexts. This capacity is ensured by the moral virtues, in particular by prudence that masters the particulars of a situation in order to direct concrete action. The prudent man must possess not only the knowledge of the universal but also knowledge of the particular. In order to indicate well the proper character of this virtue, St. Thomas Aquinas is not afraid to say: "If he should happen to have only one of the two kinds of knowledge, it is preferable that it be knowledge of the particular realities that more closely affect the action"[58]. With prudence it is a matter of: penetrating a contingency that always remains mysterious to reason; modelling itself on reality in as exact a manner as possible; assimilating the multiplicity of circumstances; and, taking as accurate an account as possible of a situation that is original and ineffable. Such an objective necessitates the numerous operations and abilities that prudence must put in place.

57. The subject, however, must not lose himself in the concrete and the particular, a fault for which "situation ethics" was criticized. He must discover the "right rule of acting" and establish an adequate norm of action. This right rule follows from preliminary principles. Here one thinks of the first principles of practical reason, but it also falls to the moral virtues to open and connaturalize both the will and the sensitive affectivity with regard to different human goods, and so to indicate to the

---

[58] Cf St. Thomas Aquinas, *Sententia libri Ethicorum*, Lib. VI, 6 (ed. Leonine, t. XLVII, 353-354): "Prudence considers not only universals, a domain in which there is no action, but must also know singulars, since it is active, i.e., a principle of acting. Action, however, regards singulars. Hence some who do not have knowledge of universals are more active regarding some particular things than those who have universal knowledge because they have experience of particular realities [...] Therefore since prudence is active reason, the prudent man must have each kind of knowledge, namely of universals and of particulars; or if he happens to have only one, it should rather be knowledge of particulars, which are closer to operation. (Prudentia enim non considerat solum universalia, in quibus non est actio; sed oportet quod cognoscat singularia, eo quod est activa, idest principium agendi. Actio autem est circa singularia. Et inde est, quod quidam non habentes scientiam universalium sunt magis activi circa aliqua particularia, quam illi qui habent universalem scientiam, eo quod sunt in aliis particularibus experti. [...] Quia igitur prudentia est ratio activa, oportet quod prudens habeat utramque notitiam, scilicet et universalium et particularium; vel, si alteram solum contingat ipsum habere, magis debet habere hanc, scilicet notitiam particularium quae sunt propinquiora operationi)".

prudent person the ends to be pursued in the midst of the flux of everyday events. It is only then that he will be able to formulate the concrete norm that applies and to imbue the given action with a ray of justice, of fortitude or of temperance. It would not be incorrect to speak here of the exercise of an "emotional intelligence"; the rational powers, without losing their specific character, are at work within the affective field, in such a way that the totality of the person is engaged in the moral action.

58. Prudence is indispensable to the moral subject because of the flexibility required to adapt universal moral principles to the diversity of situations. But this flexibility does not authorize one to see prudence as a way of easy compromise with regard to moral values. On the contrary, it is through the decisions of prudence that the concrete requirements of moral truth are expressed for a subject. Prudence is a necessary element in the exercise of one's authentic moral obligation.

59. This is an approach which, within a pluralist society like our own, takes on an importance that cannot be underestimated without considerable harm. Indeed, it takes account of the fact that moral science cannot furnish an acting subject with a norm to be applied adequately and almost automatically to concrete situations; only the conscience of the subject, the judgment of his practical reason, can formulate the immediate norm of action. But at the same time, this approach does not abandon conscience to mere subjectivity: it aims at having the subject acquire the intellectual and affective dispositions which allow him to be open to moral truth, so that his judgment may be adequate. Natural law could not, therefore, be presented as an already established set of rules that impose themselves *a priori* on the moral subject; rather, it is a source of objective inspiration for the deeply personal process of making a decision.

CHAPTER 3: THE THEORETICAL FOUNDATIONS OF THE NATURAL LAW

3.1. From experience to theory

60. The spontaneous grasp of fundamental ethical values, which are expressed in the precepts of the natural law, constitutes the point of departure of the process that then leads the moral subject to the judgment of conscience, in which he formulates the moral requirements that impose themselves on him in his concrete situation. It is the task of the theologian and of the philosopher to reflect on this experience of grasping the first principles of ethics, in order to test its value and base it on reason. The recognition of these philosophical or theological foundations does not, however, condition the spontaneous adherence to common values. In fact, the moral subject can put into practice the orientations of natural law without being capable – by reason of his particular intellectual formation – of explicitly discerning their ultimate theoretical foundations.

61. The philosophical justification of natural law presents two levels of coherence and depth. The idea of a natural law is justified first of all on the level of the reflective observation of the anthropological constants that characterize a successful humanization of the person and a harmonious social life. Thoughtful experience, conveyed by the wisdom traditions, by philosophies or by human sciences, allows us to determine some of the conditions required so that each one may best display his human capacities in his personal and communal life[59]. In this way, certain behaviours are recognized as expressing an exemplary excellence in the manner of living and of realizing one's humanity. They define the main lines of a properly moral ideal of a virtuous life "according to nature", that is to say, in conformity with the profound nature of the human subject[60].

---

[59] For example, experimental psychology emphasizes the importance of the active presence of the parents of both sexes for the harmonious development of the child's personality, and the decisive role of paternal authority for the construction of the child's identity. Political history suggests that the participation of all in decisions that regard the totality of the community is generally a factor of social peace and political stability.

[60] At this first level, the expression of the natural law sometimes abstracts from an explicit reference to God. Certainly the openness to transcendence is part of the virtuous behaviour that one rightly expects from a fully developed human being, but God is not yet necessarily recognized as the foundation and the source of the natural law, nor as the last end that

62. Nevertheless, only the recognition of the metaphysical dimension of the real can give to natural law its full and complete philosophical justification. In fact metaphysics allows for understanding that the universe does not have in itself its own ultimate reason for being, and manifests the fundamental structure of the real: the distinction between God, subsistent being himself, and the other beings placed by him in existence. God is the Creator, the free and transcendent source of all other beings. From him, these beings receive, "with measure, number and weight" (*Wis* 11:20), existence according to a nature that defines them. Creatures are therefore the epiphany of a personal creative wisdom, of an originating Logos who expresses and manifests himself in them. "Every creature is a divine word, because it speaks of God", writes St. Bonaventure[61].

63. The Creator is not only the principle of creatures but also the transcendent end towards which they tend by nature. Thus creatures are animated by a dynamism that carries them to fulfil themselves, each in its own way, in the union with God. This dynamism is transcendent, to the extent to which it proceeds from the eternal law, i.e., from the plan of divine providence that exists in the mind of the Creator[62]. But it is also immanent, because it is not imposed on creatures from without, but is inscribed in their very nature. Purely material creatures realize spontaneously the law of their being, while spiritual creatures realize it

---

mobilizes and arranges in a hierarchy the different kinds of virtuous behaviour. This lack of an explicit recognition of God as the ultimate moral norm seems to prevent the "empirical" approach to the natural law from being constituted as properly moral doctrine.

[61] ST. BONAVENTURE, *Commentarius in Ecclesiasten*, cap. 1 (*Opera omnia*, VI, ed. Quaracchi, 1893, p. 16): "Verbum divinum est omnis creatura, quia Deum loquitur".

[62] Cf. ST. THOMAS AQUINAS, *Summa theologiae, Ia-IIae*, q. 91, a. 1: "Law is nothing other than a certain dictate of practical reason in the leader who governs some perfect community. Now it is evident, supposing that the world is ruled by divine providence, [...] that the whole community of the universe is governed by the divine reason. Hence the very idea [...] of the governing of things in God the ruler of the universe, has the aspect of law. And since the divine reason's conception of things is not subject to time, but is eternal [...] therefore it is necessary to call this kind of law eternal. (Nihil est aliud lex quam quoddam dictamen practicae rationis in principe qui gubernat aliquam communitatem perfectam. Manifestum est autem, supposito quod mundus divina providentia regatur [...], quod tota communitas universi gubernatur ratione divina. Et ideo ipsa ratio gubernationis rerum in Deo sicut in principe universitatis existens, legis habet rationem. Et quia divina ratio nihil concipit ex tempore, sed habet aeternum conceptum [...] ; inde est quod huiusmodi legem oportet dicere aeternam).

in a personal manner. In fact, they interiorize the dynamisms that define them and freely orient them towards their own complete realization. They formulate them to themselves, as fundamental norms of their moral action – this is the natural law properly stated – and they strive to realize them freely. The natural law is therefore defined as a participation in the eternal law[63]. It is mediated, on the one hand, by the inclinations of nature, expressions of the creative wisdom, and, on the other hand, by the light of human reason which interprets them and is itself a created participation in the light of the divine intelligence. Ethics is thus presented as a "participated theonomy"[64].

3.2. Nature, person and freedom

64. The notion of nature is particularly complex and is not at all univocal. In philosophy, the Greek thought of *physis* enjoys a role as a matrix. In it, nature refers to the principle of the specific ontological identity of a subject, i.e., its essence which is defined by an ensemble of stable, intelligible characteristics. This essence takes the name of nature above all when it is envisaged as the internal principle of movement that orients the subject towards its fulfilment. Far from referring to a static given, the notion of nature signifies the real dynamic principle of the homogeneous development of the subject and of its specific activities. The notion of nature was formed at first to think about material and perceptible realities, but it is not limited to this "physical" domain and it applies analogically to spiritual realities.

65. The idea that beings possess a nature is convincing as an explanation of the immanent finality of beings and of the regularity that is perceived in

---

[63] Cf Ibid., *Ia-IIae*, q. 91, a. 2: "Unde patet quod lex naturalis nihil aliud est quam participatio legis aeternae in rationali creatura".

[64] JOHN PAUL II, Encyclical, *Veritatis splendor*, n. 41. The teaching of the natural law as the foundation of ethics is by right accessible to human reason. History attests to this. But, in fact, this teaching has only attained its full maturity under the influence of Christian revelation. This is, first of all, because the comprehension of the natural law as participation in the eternal law is closely linked to a metaphysics of creation. Now, although this metaphysics is by right accessible to philosophical reason, it was not truly brought to light and made explicit except under the influence of biblical monotheism. And then, because revelation, for example through the Decalogue, explains, confirms, purifies and perfects the fundamental principles of the natural law.

their way of acting and reacting[65]. To consider beings as natures, therefore, amounts to recognizing in them a proper consistency and affirming that they are relatively autonomous centres in the order of being and of acting, and not simply illusions or temporary constructions of the consciousness. These "natures" are, however, not closed ontological unities, locked in themselves and simply placed one alongside the other. They act upon each other, and have complex relations of causality among themselves. In the spiritual order, persons weave intersubjective relations. Natures therefore form a network, and in the last analysis, an order, i.e., a series unified by reference to a principle[66].

66. With Christianity, the *physis* of the ancients is rethought and integrated into a broader and more profound vision of reality. On the one hand, the God of Christian revelation is not a simple component of the universe, an element of the great All of nature. On the contrary, he is the transcendent and free Creator of the universe. In fact the finite universe cannot be its own foundation, but points to the mystery of an infinite God, who out of pure love created it *ex nihilo* and remains free to intervene in the course of nature whenever he wills. On the other hand, the transcendent mystery of God is reflected in the mystery of the human person as an image of God. The human person is capable of knowledge and of love; he is endowed with freedom, capable of entering into communion with others and called by God to a destiny that transcends the finalities of physical nature. He fulfils himself in a free and gratuitous relationship of love with God that is realized in a history.

---

[65] Does not the theory of evolution, which tends to reduce species to a precarious and provisory equilibrium in the flux of becoming, put radically into question the very concept of nature? In fact, whatever its value on the level of empirical biological description, the notion of species responds to a permanent requirement of the philosophical explanation of living beings. Only recourse to a formal specificity, irreducible to the sum of the material properties, allows one to give an account of the intelligibility of the internal functioning of a living organism considered as a coherent whole.

[66] The theological doctrine of original sin strongly underlines the real unity of human nature. This cannot be reduced to a simple abstraction, nor to a sum of individual realities. It indicates rather a totality that embraces all human beings who share the same destiny. The simple fact of being born (*nasci*) puts us in enduring relations of solidarity with all other human beings.

67. By its insistence on freedom as the condition of man's response to the initiative of God's love, Christianity has contributed in a decisive way towards giving the notion of person its rightful place in philosophical discourse, in a manner which has had a decisive influence on ethical teachings. Moreover, the theological exploration of the Christian mystery has led to a very significant deepening of the philosophical theme of the person. On the one hand, the notion of person serves to designate, in their distinction, the Father, the Son, and the Spirit, within the infinite mystery of the one divine nature. On the other hand, the person is the point in which, with respect to the distinction and distance between the two natures, divine and human, the ontological unity of the God-man, Jesus Christ, is established. In the Christian theological tradition, the person presents two complementary aspects. On the one hand, according to the definition of Boethius, taken up again by scholastic theology, the person is an "individual substance (subsistent) of a rational nature"[67]. It refers to the uniqueness of an ontological subject who, being of a spiritual nature, enjoys a dignity and an autonomy that is manifested in self-consciousness and in free dominion over his actions. Furthermore, the person is manifested in his capacity to enter into relation: he displays his action in the order of intersubjectivity and of communion in love.

68. Person is not opposed to nature. On the contrary, nature and person are two notions that complement one another. On the one hand, every human person is a unique realization of human nature understood in a metaphysical sense. On the other hand, the human person, in the free choices by which he responds in the concrete of his "here and now" to his unique and transcendent vocation, assumes the orientations given by his nature. In fact, nature puts in place the conditions for the exercise of freedom and indicates an orientation for the choices that the person must make. Examining the intelligibility of his nature, the person thus discovers the ways of his own fulfilment.

---

[67] Boethius, *Contra Eutychen et Nestorium*, c. 3 (PL 64, col. 1344): "Persona est rationalis naturae individua substantia". Cf. St. BONAVENTURE, *Commentaria in librum I Sententiarum*, d. 25, a. 1, q. 2; St. THOMAS AQUINAS, *Summa theologiae, Ia,* q. 29, a. 1.

3.3. Nature, man and God: from harmony to conflict

69. The concept of natural law presupposes the idea that nature is for man the bearer of an ethical message and is an implicit moral norm that human reason actualizes. The vision of the world within which the doctrine of natural law developed and still finds its meaning today, implies therefore the reasoned conviction that there exists a harmony among the three realities: God, man, and nature. In this perspective, the world is perceived as an intelligible whole, unified by the common reference of the beings that compose it to a divine originating principle, to a *Logos*. Beyond the impersonal and immanent Logos discovered by stoicism and presupposed by the modern sciences of nature, Christianity affirms that there is a *Logos* who is personal, transcendent and creator. "It is not the elements of the universe, the laws of matter, which ultimately govern the world and mankind, but a personal God who governs the stars, that is, the universe; it is not the laws of matter and of evolution that have the final say, but reason, will, love – a Person"[68]. The personal divine *Logos*, the Wisdom and Word of God, is not only the origin and transcendent, intelligible exemplar of the universe, but also the one who maintains it in a harmonious unity and leads it to its end [69]. By the dynamisms that the creator Word has inscribed in the innermost part of beings, he orients them to their full realization. This dynamic orientation is none other than the divine government that realizes within time the plan of divine providence, i.e., the eternal law.

70. Every creature, in its own manner, participates in the *Logos*. Man, since he is defined by reason or *logos*, participates in it in an eminent manner. In fact, by his reason, he is capable of freely interiorizing the divine intentions manifested in the nature of things. He formulates them for himself under the form of a moral law that inspires and orients his action. In this perspective, man is not "the other" in relation to nature. On

---

[68] BENEDICT XVI, Encyclical *Spe salvi*, n. 5.

[69] Cf. also ST. ATHANASIUS OF ALEXANDRIA, *Traité contre les paiens*, 42 (*Sources chrétiennes*, 18, p.195): "As a musician who has just tuned his lyre, puts together by his art the low notes with the high notes, the middle notes with the others, in order to execute a single melody, so the Wisdom of God, the Word, holding the whole universe like a lyre, unites the beings of the air with those of the earth, the beings of heaven with those of the air; combines the whole with the parts; leads all by his command and his will; thus he produces, in beauty and harmony, a single world and a single order of the world".

the contrary, he maintains with the cosmos a bond of familiarity founded on a common participation in the divine *Logos*.

71. For various historical and cultural reasons, which are linked in particular to the evolution of ideas during the late Middle Ages, this vision of the world has lost its cultural supremacy. The nature of things ceased being law for modern man and is no longer a reference point for ethics. On the metaphysical level, the change from thinking about the univocity of being to thinking about the analogy of being, which was then followed by nominalism, have undermined the foundations of the doctrine of creation as a participation in the *Logos*, a doctrine that gives an explanation of a certain unity between man and nature. The nominalist universe of William of Ockham is thus reduced to a juxtaposition of individual realities without depth, since every real universal, i.e., every principle of communion among beings, is denounced as a linguistic illusion. On the anthropological level, the development of voluntarism and the correlative exaltation of subjectivity, defined by the freedom of indifference with respect to every natural inclination, have created a gulf between the human subject and nature. From that point on, some people deemed that human freedom is essentially the power to count as nothing what man is by nature. The subject should therefore not attribute any meaning to that which he has not personally chosen and should decide for himself what it is to be a human being. Man, therefore, comes to understand himself more and more as a "denatured animal", an anti-natural being who affirms himself to the extent to which he opposes himself to nature. Culture, proper to man, is then defined not as a humanization or a transfiguration of nature by the spirit, but as a pure and simple negation of nature. The principal result of these developments has been the split of the real into three separate, indeed opposed spheres: nature, human subjectivity, and God.

72. With the eclipse of the metaphysics of being, which alone is able to give the foundation of reason to the differentiated unity of spirit and of material reality, and with the rise of voluntarism, the realm of spirit has been radically opposed to the realm of nature. Nature is no longer considered as an epiphany of the *Logos*, but as "the other" of the spirit. It is reduced to the sphere of corporality and of strict necessity, and of a corporality without depth, since the world of bodies is identified with extension, certainly regulated by intelligible mathematical laws, but stripped of

every immanent teleology or finality. Cartesian physics, then Newtonian physics, have spread the image of an inert matter, which passively obeys the laws of universal determinism that the Divine Spirit imposes on it and which human reason can perfectly know and master[70]. Only man can infuse sense and design into this amorphous and meaningless mass that he manipulates for his own ends with technical skill. Nature ceases being a teacher of life and of wisdom, in order to become the place where the Promethean power of man is asserted. This vision seems to place great value on human freedom, but, in fact, by opposing freedom and nature, it deprives human freedom of every objective norm for its exercise. It leads to the idea of an entirely arbitrary human creation of values, indeed to nihilism, pure and simple.

73. In this context, in which nature no longer contains any immanent teleological rationality and seems to have lost all affinity or kinship with the world of spirit, the passage from knowledge of the structures of being to moral duty which seems to derive from it becomes effectively impossible and falls under the criticism of "naturalistic fallacy" denounced by David Hume and then by George Edward Moore in his *Principia Ethica* (1903). The good is actually disconnected from being and from truth. Ethics is separated from metaphysics.

74. The evolution of the understanding of the relationship of man to nature also finds expression in the resurgence of a radical anthropological dualism that opposes spirit and body, since the body is in some way the "nature" in each of us[71]. This dualism is manifested in the refusal to recognize any human and ethical meaning in the natural inclinations that precede the choices of the individual reason. The body, judged a

---

[70] The *physis* of the ancients, taking note of the existence of a certain non-being (matter), preserved the contingency of earthly realities and put up a resistance to the pretensions of human reason to impose on the totality of reality a purely rational deterministic order. Thus, it left open the possibility of an effective action of human freedom in the world.

[71] Cf. JOHN PAUL II, *Letter to Families*, n. 19: "The philosopher who enunciated the principle of 'Cogito, ergo sum', 'I think, therefore I am', also impressed on the modern concept of man its distinctive dualistic character. It is the distinctive feature of rationalism to draw a radical opposition in man between spirit and body, and between body and spirit. On the contrary, man is a person in the unity of his body and his spirit. The body can never be reduced to mere matter: it is a spiritualized body, just as man's spirit is so closely united to the body that he can be described as an embodied spirit".

reality external to subjectivity, becomes a pure "having" or "possession", an object manipulated by technical skill according to the interests of the individual subjectivity[72].

75. Furthermore, on account of the emergence of a metaphysical conception in which human and divine action are in competition with each another – since they are conceived in a univocal fashion and placed, wrongly, on the same level – the legitimate affirmation of the autonomy of the human subject leads to the exclusion of God from the sphere of human subjectivity. Every reference to something normative coming from God or from nature as an expression of God's wisdom, that is to say, every "heteronomy" is perceived as a threat to the subject's autonomy. The notion of natural law thus appears as incompatible with the authentic dignity of the subject.

3.4. Ways towards a reconciliation

76. To give the notion of the natural law all its meaning and strength as the foundation of a universal ethic, a perspective of wisdom needs to be promoted, belonging properly to the metaphysical order, and capable of simultaneously including God, the cosmos and the human person, in order to reconcile them in the analogical unity of being, thanks to the idea of creation as participation.

77. It is above all essential to develop a non-competitive conception of the connection between divine causality and the free activity of the human subject. The human subject achieves fulfilment by inserting himself

---

[72] The ideology of *gender*, which denies all anthropological or moral significance to the natural difference of the sexes, is inscribed in this dualistic perspective. Cf. Congregation for the Doctrine of the Faith, *Letter to the Bishops of the Catholic Church on the Collaboration of Men and Women in the Church and in the World*, n. 2: "In order to avoid the domination of one sex or the other, their differences tend to be denied, viewed as mere effects of historical and cultural conditioning. In this leveling, physical difference, termed sex, is minimized, while the purely cultural element, termed gender, is emphasized to the maximum and held to be primary. [...] While the immediate roots of this second tendency are found in the context of the question of woman, its deeper motivation must be sought in the attempt of the human person to be freed from one's biological conditioning. According to this anthropological perspective, human nature itself does not possess characteristics that impose themselves in an absolute manner: all persons can and ought to constitute themselves as they like, since they are free from every predetermination linked to their essential constitution.

freely into the providential action of God and not by opposing himself to this action. It is his prerogative to discover with his reason the profound dynamisms that define his nature, and then to accept and direct these dynamisms freely to their fulfilment. In fact, human nature is defined by an entire ensemble of dynamisms, tendencies and internal orientations within which freedom arises. Freedom actually presupposes that the human will is "activated" by the natural desire for the good and for the last end. Free will is exercised then in the choice of the finite objects that allow the attainment of this end. As regards these goods, which exercise an attraction that does not determine the will, the person retains mastery of his choice by reason of an innate openness to the absolute Good. Freedom is therefore not an absolute creator of itself, but is rather an eminent property of every human subject.

78. A philosophy of nature, which takes note of the intelligible depth of the sensible world, and especially a metaphysics of creation, allow then for the surmounting of the dualistic and Gnostic temptation of abandoning nature to moral insignificance. From this point of view, it is important to go beyond the reductionist perspective on nature which is inculcated by the dominant technical culture, in order to rediscover the moral message borne in nature, as a work of the *Logos*.

79. The rehabilitation of nature and of corporality in ethics, however, could not be the equivalent of any kind of "physicalism". In fact, some modern presentations of natural law have seriously failed to recognize the necessary integration of natural inclinations into the unity of the person. Neglecting to consider the unity of the human person, they absolutize the natural inclinations of the different "parts" of human nature, juxtaposing these inclinations without placing them in a hierarchy and omitting to integrate them into the unity of the overall, personal plan of the subject. As John Paul II explains, "natural inclinations take on moral relevance only insofar as they refer to the human person and to his authentic fulfilment"[73]. Today, therefore, it is important to hold fast to two things simultaneously. On the one hand, the human subject is not a collection or juxtaposition of diverse and autonomous natural inclinations, but a substantial and personal whole, who has the vocation to respond to the

---

[73] JOHN PAUL II, Encyclical *Veritatis splendor*, n. 50.

love of God and to unify himself by accepting his orientation towards a last end that places in hierarchical order the partial goods manifested by the various natural tendencies. This unification of natural tendencies in accordance with the higher ends of the spirit, i.e., this humanization of the dynamisms inscribed in human nature, does not in any way represent a violence done to them. On the contrary, it is the fulfilment of a promise already inscribed in them[74]. For example, the high spiritual value that the gift of self in mutual spousal love represents is already inscribed in the very nature of the sexual body, which finds its ultimate reason for being in this spiritual fulfilment. On the other hand, in this organic whole, each part preserves a proper and irreducible meaning, which must be taken into account by reason in the elaboration of the overall mission of the human person. The doctrine of the natural moral law must, therefore, maintain at the same time both the central role of reason in the actualization of a properly human plan of life, and the consistency and the proper meaning of pre-rational natural dynamisms[75].

80. The moral significance of the pre-rational natural dynamisms appears in full light in the teaching concerning sins against nature. Certainly, every sin is against nature insofar as it is opposed to right reason and hinders the authentic development of the human person. However, some behaviours are described in a special way as sins against nature to the extent that they contradict more directly the objective meaning of the natural dynamisms that the person must take up into the unity of

---

[74] The duty to humanize the nature in man is inseparable from the duty to humanize external nature. This morally justifies the immense effort of human beings to emancipate themselves from the constraints of physical nature to the degree to which these hinder the development of properly human values. The struggle against disease, the prevention of hostile natural phenomena, the improvement of living conditions are in themselves works that attest to the greatness of man called to fill the earth and to subdue it (cf. *Gen* 1:28). Cf. Pastoral Constitution *Gaudium et spes*, n. 57.

[75] Reacting to the danger of physicalism and rightly insisting on the decisive role of reason in the elaboration of the natural law, some contemporary theories of natural law neglect, indeed reject, the moral significance of the pre-rational natural dynamisms. The natural law would be called "natural" only in reference to reason, which would define the whole nature of man. To obey the natural law would therefore be reduced to acting in a rational manner, i.e., to applying to the totality of behaviours a univocal ideal of rationality generated by practical reason alone. This amounts to wrongly identifying the rationality of the natural law with the rationality of human reason alone, without taking into account the rationality immanent in nature.

his moral life[76]. So, deliberately chosen suicide goes against the natural inclination to preserve and make fruitful one's own existence. Thus some sexual practices are directly opposed to the reproductive finalities inscribed in the sexual body of man. By this very fact, they also contradict the interpersonal values that a responsible and fully human sexual life must promote.

81. The risk of absolutizing nature, reduced to its purely physical or biological component, and of neglecting its intrinsic vocation to be integrated into a spiritual project, is a threat in some radical tendencies of the ecological movement today. The irresponsible exploitation of nature by human agents who seek only economic profit and the dangers that this exploitation poses to the biosphere rightly cry out to consciences. However, "*deep ecology*" represents an excessive reaction. It extols a supposed equality of living species, to the point that it no longer recognizes any particular role for man, paradoxically undermining the responsibility of man for the biosphere of which he is a part. In a still more radical manner, some have come to consider man as a destructive virus that would supposedly strike a blow at the integrity of nature, and they refuse him any meaning and value in the biosphere. And so one arrives at a new type of totalitarianism that excludes human existence in its specificity and condemns legitimate human progress.

82. There cannot be an adequate response to the complex questions of ecology except within the framework of a deeper understanding of the natural law, which places value on the connection between the human person, society, culture, and the equilibrium of the bio-physical sphere in which the human person is incarnate. An integral ecology must promote what is specifically human, all the while valuing the world of nature in its physical and biological integrity. In fact, even if man, as a moral being who searches for the ultimate truth and the ultimate good, transcends his own immediate environment, he does so by accepting the special mission of keeping watch over the natural world, living in harmony with it, and defending vital values without which neither human life nor the biosphere

---

[76] Cf. St. Thomas Aquinas, *Summa theologiae, IIa-IIae*, q. 154, a. 11. The moral evaluation of sins against nature should take into account not only their objective gravity but also the subjective dispositions – often attenuating – of those who commit them.

of this planet can be maintained[77]. This integral ecology summons every human being and every community to a new responsibility. It is inseparable from a global political orientation respectful of the requirements of the natural law.

---

[77] Cf. *Gen* 2:15.

CHAPTER 4: NATURAL LAW AND THE CITY [πόλις]

4.1. The person and the common good

83. Turning to the political order of society, we enter into the space regulated by norms or laws. In fact, such norms appear from the moment in which persons enter in relation. The passage from person to society sheds light on the essential distinction between natural law and the norm of natural justice.

84. The person is at the centre of the political and social order because he is an end and not a means. The person is a social being by nature, not by choice or in virtue of a pure contractual convention. In order to flourish as a person, he needs the structure of relations that he forms with other persons. He thus finds himself at the centre of a network formed by concentric circles: the family, the sphere of life and work, the neighbourhood community, the nation, and finally humanity[78]. The person draws from each of these circles the elements necessary for his own growth, and at the same time he contributes to their perfection.

85. By the fact that human beings have the vocation to live in society with others, they have in common an ensemble of goods to pursue and values to defend. This is what is called the "common good". If the person is an end in himself, the end of society is to promote, consolidate and develop its common good. The search for the common good allows the city to mobilize the energies of all its members. At a first level, the common good can be understood as the ensemble of conditions that allow a person to be a more human person[79]. While being articulated in its external aspects – the economy, security, social justice, education, access to employment, spiritual searching, and other things – the common good is always a human good[80]. At a second level, the common good is that which assigns an end to the political order and to the city itself. The good of all and of

---

[78] Cf. VATICAN COUNCIL II, Pastoral Constitution *Gaudium et spes*, n. 73-74. *The Catechism of the Catholic Church*, n. 1882, clarifies that "certain societies, such as the family and the civic community, correspond more immediately to the nature of man".

[79] Cf. JOHN XXIII, Encyclical *Mater et magistra*, n. 65; VATICAN COUNCIL II, Pastoral Constitution, *Gaudium et spes*, n. 26 § 1; Declaration *Dignitatis humanae*, n. 6.

[80] Cf. JOHN XXIII, Encyclical *Pacem in terris*, n. 55.

each one in particular, it expresses the communal dimension of the human good. Societies can be defined by the type of common good that they intend to promote. In fact, if it concerns the essential requirements of the common good of every society, the vision of the common good evolves with the societies themselves, according to conceptions of the person, justice, and the role of public power.

4.2. The natural law, measure of the political order

86. The organization of society in view of the common good of its members responds to the requirements of the social nature of the person. The natural law then appears as the normative horizon in which the political order is called to move. It defines the ensemble of values that appear as humanizing for a society. As soon as we are in the social and political sphere, values can no longer be of a private, ideological or confessional nature: they concern all citizens. They do not express a vague consensus among citizens, but instead are based on the requirements of their common humanity. So that society may correctly fulfil its own mission of serving the person, it must promote the realization of the person's natural inclinations. The person is therefore prior to society, and society is humanizing only if it responds to the expectations inscribed in the person insofar as he is a social being.

87. This natural order of society at the service of the person is indicated, according to the social doctrine of the Church, by four values that follow from the natural inclinations of the human being and which delineate the contours of the common good that society must pursue, namely: freedom, truth, justice, and solidarity[81]. These four values correspond to the requirements of an ethical order in conformity with the natural law. If one of these is lacking, the city will tend towards anarchy or the rule of the strongest. Freedom is the first condition of a humanly acceptable political order. Without the liberty to follow one's conscience, express one's own opinions and pursue one's own plans, there is no human city, even if the pursuit of private goods must always be related to the promotion of the common good of the city. Without the search and respect for truth, there is not a society but a dictatorship of the strongest.

---

[81] Cf. Ibid., n. 37; PONTIFICAL COUNCIL FOR JUSTICE AND PEACE, *Compendium of the Social Doctrine of the Church*, n. 192-203.

Truth, which is not the property of anyone, is alone capable of bringing all human beings together in view of pursuing common objectives. If it is not truth that imposes itself, it is the most clever who imposes "his" truth. Without justice there is no society, but the reign of violence. Justice is the highest good that the city can procure. It means that what is just is always sought, and that the law is applied with attention to the particular case, since equity is the highest part of justice. Finally, it is necessary for society to be regulated by a kind of solidarity which assures mutual assistance and responsibility for others, as well as the use of society's goods in response to the needs of all.

4.3. From natural law to the norm of natural justice

88. Natural law (*lex naturalis*) becomes the norm of natural justice (*ius naturale*) when one considers the relations of justice among human beings: relations among physical and moral persons, relations between persons and the public authority, relations of everyone with the positive law. We pass from the anthropological category of the natural law to the juridical and political category of the organization of the city. The norm of natural justice is the inherent standard of the right interaction among members of society. It is the rule and immanent measure of interpersonal and social human relations.

89. This norm is not arbitrary: the requirements of justice, which flow from the natural law, are prior to the formulation and enactment of the norm. It is not the norm which determines what is just. Nor is politics arbitrary: the norms of justice do not result only from a contract established among men, but arise first from the very nature of the human being. The norm of natural justice anchors human law in the natural law. It is the horizon from which the human legislator must take his bearings when he issues rules in his mission to serve the common good. In this sense, it honours the natural law, inherent in the human person's humanity. By contrast, when the norm of natural justice is denied, it is the mere will of the legislator that is the basis of law. Then, the legislator is no longer the interpreter of what is just and good, but has arrogated to himself the prerogative of being the ultimate criterion of what is just.

90. The norm of natural justice is never a standard that is fixed once and for all. It results from an appreciation of the changing situations in which people live. It articulates the judgment of practical reason in its estimation of what is just. Such a norm, as the juridical expression of the natural law in the political order, thus appears as the measure of the just relations among the members of the community.

4.4. The norm of natural justice and positive law

91. Positive law must strive to carry out the norm of natural justice. It does this either by way of conclusions (natural justice forbids homicide, positive law prohibits abortion), or by way of determination (natural justice prescribes that the guilty be punished, positive penal law determines the punishments to be applied in each category of crime)[82]. Inasmuch as they truly derive from the norm of natural justice and therefore from the eternal law, positive human laws are binding in conscience. In the opposite case, they are not binding. "If the law is not just, it is not even a law"[83]. Positive laws can and even must change to remain faithful to their purpose. In fact, on the one hand, human reason makes progress little by little, becoming more aware of what is most suitable to the good of the community, and on the other hand, the historical conditions of the life of societies change (for better or for worse) and the laws must adapt to this[84]. Thus the legislator must determine what is just in concrete historical situations[85].

---

[82] Cf. St. Thomas Aquinas, *Summa theologiae, Ia-IIae,* q. 95, a. 2.

[83] St. Augustine, *De libero arbitrio,* I, V, 11 (*Corpus christianorum,* series latina, 29, 217): "In fact a law that is not just does not seem to me to be a law"; St. Thomas Aquinas, *Summa theologiae, Ia-IIae,* q. 93, a. 3, ad 2: "Human law has the nature of law insofar as it in accord with right reason, and in this respect it is evident that it derives from the eternal law. But insofar as it departs from reason, it is called an unjust law, and does not have the nature of law, but rather of a certain violence. (Lex humana intantum habet rationem legis, inquantum est secundum rationem rectam, et secundum hoc manifestum est quod a lege aetera derivatur. Inquantum vero a ratione recedit, sic dicitur lex iniqua, et sic non habet rationem legis, sed magis violentiae cuiusdam)"; *Ia-IIae,* q. 95, a. 2: "Consequently every law made by men has just so much of the nature of law to the extent that it is derived from the natural law. But if in some matter it deflects from the natural law, then it will not be law, but a perversion of law.(Unde omnis lex humanitus posita intantum habet de ratione legis, inquantum a lege naturae derivatur. Si vero in aliquo a lege naturali discordet, iam non erit lex sed legis corruptio).

[84] Cf St. Thomas Aquinas, *Summa theologiae Ia-IIae,* q. 97, a. 1.

[85] For Saint Augustine, the legislator, to do a good work, must consult the eternal law; cf. St. Augustine, *De vera religione,* XXXI, 58 (*Corpus christianorum,* series latina, 32, 225):

92. The norms of natural justice are thus the measures of human relationships prior to the will of the legislator. They are given from the moment that human beings live in society. They express what is naturally just, prior to any legal formulation. The norms of natural justice are expressed in a particular way in the subjective rights of the human person, such as the right to respect for one's own life, the right to the integrity of one's person, the right to religious liberty, the right to freedom of thought, the right to start a family and to educate one's children according to one's convictions, the right to associate with others, the right to participate in the life of the community, etc. These rights, to which contemporary thought attributes great importance, do not have their source in the fluctuating desires of individuals, but rather in the very structure of human beings and their humanizing relations. The rights of the human person emerge therefore from the order of justice that must reign in relations among human beings. To acknowledge these natural rights of man means to acknowledge the objective order of human relations based on the natural law.

4.5. The political order is not the eschatological order

93. In the history of human societies, the political order has often been understood as the reflection of a transcendent and divine order. Thus the ancient cosmologies provided the foundation and justification for political theologies in which the sovereign ensured the link between the cosmos and the human universe. It was a question of bringing the universe of men into the pre-established harmony of the world. With the appearance of biblical monotheism, the universe was understood as obedient to the laws which the Creator gave it. The order of the city is achieved when the laws of God are respected, laws which moreover are inscribed in the human heart. For a long time, forms of theocracy were able to prevail in societies organized according to principles and values drawn from their holy books. There was no distinction between the sphere of religious revelation and the sphere of the organization of the city. But the Bible

"The legislator of temporal laws, if he is a good and wise man, consults that eternal law, about which it is given to no soul to judge, so that, according to its immutable rules, he may discern what should be commanded and what should be forbidden at a given time". In a secularized society, in which everyone does not recognize the mark of this eternal law, it is the search for, the safeguarding of, and the expression of the norm of natural justice by means of positive law that guarantee its legitimacy.

desacralized human authority, even if centuries of theocratic osmosis – in Christian contexts as well – obscured the essential distinction between the political order and the religious order. In this regard, one must carefully distinguish the situation of the first covenant, in which the divine law given by God was also the law of the people of Israel, from that of the new covenant, which introduces the distinction and the relative autonomy of the religious and political orders.

94. The biblical revelation invites humanity to consider that the order of creation is a universal order in which all of humanity participates, and that this order is accessible to reason. When we speak of natural law, it is a question of this order willed by God and grasped by human reason. The Bible formulates the distinction between the order of creation and the order of grace, to which faith in Christ gives access. The order of the city is not this definitive or eschatological order. The domain of politics is not that of the heavenly city, a gratuitous gift of God. It concerns the imperfect and transitory order in which human beings live, all the while advancing towards their fulfilment in what lies beyond history. According to St. Augustine, the distinctive characteristic of the earthly city is to be mixed: the just and unjust, believers and unbelievers rub shoulders together[86]. They must temporarily live together according to the requirements of their nature and the capacity of their reason.

95. The state, therefore, cannot set itself up as the bearer of ultimate meaning. It cannot impose a global ideology, nor a religion (even secular), nor one way of thinking. In civil society religious organizations, philosophies and spiritualities take charge of the domain of ultimate meaning; they must contribute to the common good, strengthen the social bond and promote the universal values that are the foundation of the political order itself. The political order is not called to transpose onto earth the kingdom of God that is to come. It can anticipate the kingdom by advances in the area of justice, solidarity, and peace. It cannot seek to establish it by force.

---

[86] Cf St. AUGUSTINE, *De civitate dei*, I, 35 (*Corpus christianorum*, series latina, 47, p. 34-35).

4.6. The political order is a temporal and rational order

96. If the political order is not the sphere of ultimate truth, it must, nevertheless, be open to the perpetual search for God, truth, and justice. The "legitimate and sound secularity of the state"[87] consists in the distinction between the supernatural order of theological faith and the political order. This latter order can never be confused with the order of grace to which all persons are called to freely adhere. It is, rather, linked to the universal human ethics inscribed in human nature. The city must thus procure for the people who compose it what is necessary for the full realization of their human life, which includes certain spiritual and religious values, as well as freedom for the citizens to make up their mind with respect to the Absolute and the highest goods. But the city, whose common good is temporal in nature, cannot procure strictly supernatural goods, which are of another order.

97. If God and all transcendence were to be excluded from the political horizon, only the power of man over man would remain. In fact, the political order has sometimes presented itself as the ultimate horizon of meaning for humanity. Totalitarian ideologies and regimes have demonstrated that such a political order, without a transcendent horizon, is not humanly acceptable. This transcendence is linked to what we call natural law.

98. The politico-religious osmosis of the past as well as the totalitarian experiences of the twentieth century have led to a healthy reaction in which the value of reason in politics is today once again valued, thus conferring a new relevance to the Aristotelian-Thomistic discourse on natural law. Politics, that is, the organization of the city and the elaboration of its collective projects, pertains to the natural order and must undertake a rational debate open to transcendence.

99. The natural law which is the basis of the social and political order does not demand the adherence of faith, but of reason. Certainly, reason itself is often obscured by passions, by contradictory interests, and prejudices. But constant reference to natural law presses for a continual purification of reason. Only in this way does the political order avoid

---

[87] Cf. Pius XII, *Address given on March 23, 1958* (AAS 25 [1958], p. 220).

the trap of the arbitrary, of particular interests, organized lying, and manipulation of minds. The reference to natural law keeps the state from yielding to the temptation to absorb civil society and to subject human beings to an ideology. It also avoids the development of the paternalistic state that deprives persons and communities of every initiative and takes responsibility away from them. Natural law contains the idea of the state, based on law, structured according to the principle of subsidiarity, respecting persons and intermediate bodies, and regulating their interactions[88].

100. The great political myths were only able to be unmasked with the introduction of the rule of rationality and the acknowledgment of the transcendence of the God of love, who forbids the worship of the earthly political order. The God of the Bible willed the order of creation so that all people, conforming themselves to the law inherent in creation, can freely search for this order, and having found it, may project onto the world the light of grace, which is its fulfilment.

---

[88] Cf Pius XI, Encyclical *Quadragesimo anno*, n. 79-80.

CHAPTER 5: JESUS CHRIST, THE FULFILMENT OF THE NATURAL LAW

101. Grace does not destroy nature but heals, strengthens, and leads it to its full realization. As a consequence, while the natural law is an expression of the reason common to all human beings and can be presented in a coherent and true manner on the philosophical level, it is not foreign to the order of grace. The demands of the natural law remain present and active in the various theological stages of salvation history through which humanity passes.

102. The plan of salvation initiated by the eternal Father is realized by the mission of the Son who gives humanity the new law, the law of the Gospel, which consists principally in the grace of the Holy Spirit acting in the hearts of believers to sanctify them. The new law aims above all to procure for human beings a participation in the Trinitarian communion of the divine persons, but at the same time takes up and realizes the natural law in an eminent manner. On the one hand, the new law recalls clearly the demands of the natural law that can be obscured by sin and by ignorance. On the other hand, by emancipating us from the law of sin, on account of which "I can will what is right, but I cannot do it" (*Rom* 7:18), the new law gives human beings the effective capacity to overcome their self-centredness in order to put fully into action the humanizing requirements of the natural law.

5.1. The incarnate *Logos*, the living Law

103. Thanks to the natural light of reason, which is a participation in the divine light, human beings are capable of scrutinizing the intelligible order of the universe so as to discover there the expression of the wisdom, beauty and goodness of the Creator. On the basis of this knowledge, they are to enter into this order by their moral action. Now, in virtue of a deeper perspective on God's plan, of which the creative act is the prelude, Scripture teaches believers that this world has been created in, by and for the *Logos*, the Word of God, the beloved Son of the Father, uncreated Wisdom, and that the world has life and subsistence in him. In fact the Son is "the image of the invisible God, the firstborn of all creation, for in him [*en auto*] all things were created, in heaven and on earth, visible and

invisible ....All things were created through him [*di'auton*] and for him [*eis auton*]. He is before all things, and in him [*en auto*] all things hold together" (*Col* 1:15-17)[89]. The Logos is therefore the key of creation. The human person, created in the image of God, bears in himself a very special imprint of this personal Logos. Consequently, he has the vocation to be conformed and assimilated to the Son, "the firstborn of many brethren" (*Rom* 8:29).

104. But by sin man has made bad use of his freedom and has turned away from the source of wisdom. By doing so, he has distorted the perception that he was able to have of the objective order of things, even on the natural level. Human beings, knowing that their works are bad, hate the light and elaborate false theories to justify their sins[90]. Thus the image of God in man is seriously obscured. Even if their nature still refers them to a fulfilment in God beyond themselves (the creature cannot pervert himself to this point of no longer perceiving the testimony that the Creator offers of himself in creation), men, in fact, are so gravely affected by sin that they do not recognize the profound meaning of the world and interpret it in terms of pleasure, money or power.

105. By his salvific incarnation, the *Logos*, assuming a human nature, restored the image of God and gave man back to himself. Thus Jesus Christ, the new Adam, brings the original plan of the Father for humanity to fulfilment and by this very fact reveals man to himself: "In reality, only in the mystery of the Incarnate Word does the mystery of man become clear. For Adam, the first man, was a figure of him who was to come, namely, Christ the Lord. Christ, the new Adam, in the very revelation of the mystery of the Father and his love, fully reveals man to man himself and makes known to him the sublimity of his vocation .... 'The image of the invisible God' (*Col* 1:15), he is the perfect man, who has restored to the sons of Adam the divine likeness deformed from the first sin onward. Because the human nature in him was assumed, not destroyed, by that very fact it has also been raised up to a sublime dignity in us too"[91]. In his person Jesus Christ, therefore, manifests an exemplary

---

[89] Cf. also *Jn* 1:3-4; 1 *Cor* 8:6; *Heb* 1:2-3.

[90] Cf. *Jn* 3:19-20; *Rom* 1:24-25.

[91] VATICAN II, Pastoral constitution, *Gaudium et spes*, n. 22; Cf. ST. IRENAEUS OF LYON,

human life, fully conformed to the natural law. He is thus the ultimate criterion for correctly discerning the authentic natural desires of man, when these are not concealed by the distortions introduced by sin and disordered passions.

106. The Incarnation of the Son was prepared by the economy of the old law, a sign of God's love for his people Israel. For some of the Fathers of the Church, one of the reasons why God gave Moses a written law was to remind human beings of the requirements of the law naturally written in their hearts, but which sin had partially obscured and erased[92]. This law, which Judaism identified with the pre-existing Wisdom that presides over the destinies of the universe[93], thus placed within the reach of human beings marked by sin the concrete practice of true wisdom, which consists in the love of God and neighbour. It contained positive liturgical and juridical precepts, but also moral prescriptions, summarized

---

Contre les hérésies, V, 16, 2 ("*Sources chrétiennes*, 153" pp. 216-217: "In times past, one properly said that man had been made in the image of God, but this did not appear, for the Word was still invisible, he in whose image man had been made: it is moreover for this reason that the likeness was easily lost. But when the Word of God became flesh, he confirmed the one and the other: he made the image appear in all its truth, by becoming himself what was his image, and he re-established the likeness in a stable manner, by making man completely like the invisible Father by means of the Word, henceforth visible".

[92] Cf. St. Augustine, *Enarrationes in Psalmos*, 1 vii, 1 (*Corpus christianorum*, series latina, 39, p. 708): "By the hand of our Creator, the Truth, has written these words in our very hearts: 'Do not do to others what you would not want done to you'. Before the law was given no one was permitted to be ignorant of this principle, so that they could be judged to whom the law was not given. But in order to prevent men from complaining that they lacked something, it was written on the tablets what they were not reading in their hearts. It is not that they did not have something written; it is that they did not want to read it. One placed, therefore, before their eyes what they would be compelled to see in their conscience. As if moved by the voice of God from without, man was compelled to look inside himself (Quandoquidem manu formatoris nostri in ipsis cordibus nostris veritas scripsit: 'Quod tibi non vis fieri, ne facias alteri'. Hoc et antequam lex daretur nemo ignorare permissus est, ut esset unde iudicarentur et quibus lex non esset data. Sed ne sibi homines aliquid defuisse quaererentur, scriptum est et in tabulis quod in cordibus non legebant. Non enim scriptum non habebant, sed legere nolebant. Oppositum est oculis eorum quod in conscientia videre cogerentur ; et quasi forinsecus admota voce Dei, ad interiora sua homo compulsus est)". Cf. St. Thomas Aquinas, *In III Sent.*, d. 37, q. 1, a. 1: "Necessarium fuit ea quae naturalis ratio dictat, quae dicuntur ad legem naturae pertinere, populo in praeceptum dari, et in scriptum redigi [...] quia per contrariam consuetudinem, qua multi in peccato praecipitabantur, jam apud multos ratio naturalis, in qua scripta erant, obtenebrata erat"; *Summa theologiae*, I-II, q. 98, a. 6.

[93] Cf. *Sir* 24:23 (Vulgate: 24:32-33).

in the Decalogue, which corresponded to the essential implications of the natural law. That is why the Christian tradition has seen in the Decalogue a privileged and always valid expression of the natural law[94].

107. Jesus Christ did not "come to abolish but to fulfil" the law (*Mt* 5:17)[95]. As is evident from the gospel texts, Jesus "taught as one who had authority, and not as the scribes" (*Mk* 1:22) and he did not hesitate to relativize, indeed to abrogate, certain particular and temporary dispositions of the law. But he also confirmed the essential content of them and, in his person, brought the practice of the law to its perfection, taking up by love the different types of precepts – moral, cultural and judicial – of the Mosaic law, which correspond to the three functions of prophet, priest, and king. St. Paul affirms that Christ is the end (*telos*) of the law (*Rom* 10:4). *Telos* has here a twofold sense. Christ is the "goal" of the law, in the sense in which the law is a pedagogical means with the calling to lead people to Christ. But also, for all those who by faith live in him from the Spirit of love, Christ "puts an end" to the positive obligations of the law added on to the requirements of the natural law[96].

108. Jesus, in effect, has highlighted in different ways the ethical primacy of charity, which inseparably unites love of God and love of neighbour[97]. Charity is the "new commandment" (*Jn* 13:34) that recapitulates the whole law and gives the key to its interpretation: "On these two commandments depend all the law and the prophets" (*Mt* 22:40). Charity also reveals the profound meaning of the golden rule. "And what you hate, do not do to anyone" (Tob 4:15) becomes with Christ the commandment to love without limit. The context in which Jesus cites the golden rule determines

---

[94] Cf. ST. THOMAS AQUINAS, *Summa theologiae*, Ia-IIae, q. 100.

[95] Byzantine liturgy of ST. JOHN CHRYSOSTOM expresses well the Christian conviction when it puts in the mouth of the priest who blesses the deacon in thanksgiving after the communion: "Christ our God, who are yourself the fulfilment of the Law and the Prophets, and have fulfilled the whole mission received from the Father, fill our hearts with joy and gladness, at all times, now and always, forever and ever. Amen".

[96] Cf. *Gal* 3,24-26: "Thus the law served as a pedagogue leading us to Christ, so that we might obtain our justification by faith. But now that faith has come, we are no longer under a pedagogue; for in Christ Jesus you are all sons of God, through faith". On the theological notion of fulfilment, cf. PONTIFICAL BIBLICAL COMMISSION, *The Jewish People and Their Sacred Scriptures in the Christian Bible*, especially n. 21.

[97] Cf. *Mt* 22: 37-40; *Mk* 12:29-31; *Lk* 10:27.

its comprehension in depth. It is found at the centre of a section that begins with the commandment: "Love your enemies, do good to those who hate you" and culminates in the exhortation "Be merciful, even as your Father is merciful"[98]. Beyond a rule of commutative justice, the golden rule takes on the form of a challenge: it invites one to take the initiative in a love that is a gift of self. The parable of the Good Samaritan is characteristic of this Christian application of the golden rule: the centre of interest passes from care of self to care for the other[99]. The beatitudes and the Sermon on the Mount make explicit the manner in which one must live the commandment of love, in the spirit of gratuity and sense of the other, elements proper to the new perspective assumed by Christian love. Thus the practice of love overcomes every closure and every limitation. It acquires a universal dimension and a matchless strength, because it renders the person capable of doing what would be impossible without love.

109. But it is especially in the mystery of his holy passion that Jesus fulfils the law of love. There, as Love incarnate, he reveals in a fully human manner what love is and what it entails: to give one's life for those whom one loves[100]. "Having loved his own who were in the world, he loved them to the end" (*Jn* 13:1). Through loving obedience to the Father, and through the desire for the Father's glory which consists in the salvation of human beings, Jesus accepts the suffering and death of the Cross on behalf of sinners. The very person of Christ, *Logos* and Wisdom incarnate, thus became the living law, the supreme norm for all Christian ethics. The *sequela Christi*, the *imitatio Christi* are the concrete ways of carrying out the law in all its dimensions.

5.2. The Holy Spirit and the new law of freedom

110. Jesus Christ is not only an ethical model to imitate, but by and in his paschal mystery, he is the Saviour who gives us the real possibility of putting the law of love into action. In fact, the paschal mystery culminates in the gift of the Holy Spirit, the Spirit of love common to the Father and the Son, who unites the disciples among themselves, to Christ and finally to the Father. By "pouring the love of God into our hearts" (*Rom* 5:5),

---

[98] Cf. *Lk* 6:27-36.

[99] Cf. *Lk* 10:25-37.

[100] Cf. *Jn* 15:13.

the Holy Spirit becomes the interior principle and the supreme rule of the action of believers. It makes them accomplish spontaneously and with discernment all the requirements of love. "Walk by the Spirit, and do not gratify the desires of the flesh" (*Gal* 5:16). Thus the promise is fulfilled: "A new heart I will give you, and a new spirit I will put within you; and I will take out of your flesh the heart of stone and give you a heart of flesh. And I will put my spirit within you, and cause you to walk in my statutes and be careful to observe my ordinances" (*Ezek* 36: 26-27)[101].

111. The grace of the Holy Spirit constitutes the principal element of the new law or law of the Gospel[102]. The preaching of the Church, the celebration of the sacraments, the measures taken by the Church to promote in her members the development of life in the Spirit are totally referred to the personal growth of every believer in the holiness of love. With the new law, which is an essentially interior law, "the perfect law, the law of liberty" (*Jas* 1:25), the desire for autonomy and freedom in the truth that is present in the human heart attains here below its most perfect realization. It is from the very core of the person inhabited by Christ and transformed by the Spirit, that his moral action springs forth[103].

---

[101] Cf. also *Jer* 3 1:33-34.

[102] Cf. St. Thomas Aquinas, *Summa theologiae, Ia-IIae*, q. 106, a. 1: "That which is most prominent in the law of the New Testament, and in which its whole power consists, is the grace of the Holy Spirit, which is given through the faith in Christ. And therefore the new law is principally the grace of the Holy Spirit, which is given to the Christian faithful. (Id autem quod est potissimum in lege novi testamenti, et in quo tota virtus eius consistit, est gratia Spiritus sancti, quae datur per fidem Christi. Et ideo principaliter lex nova est ipsa gratia Spiritus sancti, quae datur Christi fidelibus)".

[103] Cf. Ibid., *Ia-IIae,* q. 108, a. 1, ad 2: "Therefore since the grace of the Holy Spirit is like an interior habit infused into us, inclining us to act rightly, it makes us do freely the things becoming to grace, and avoid the things opposed to grace. Thus the new law is called the law of freedom in two ways. In one way, because it does not compel us to do or avoid certain things unless they are of themselves necessary for or opposed to salvation, which are commanded or forbidden by the law. Second, because it makes us fulfil precepts or prohibitions of this kind freely, insofar as we fulfil them from the interior impulse of grace. And on account of these two things the new law is called the "law of perfect freedom" in *Jas* 1:25. (Quia igitur gratia Spiritus sancti est sicut habitus nobis infusus inclinans nos ad recte operandum, facit nos libere operari ea quae conveniunt gratiae, et vitare ea quae gratiae repugnant. Sic igitur lex nova dicitur lex libertatis dupliciter. Uno modo, quia non arctat nos ad facienda vel vitanda aliqua, nisi quae de se sunt vel necessaria vel repugnantia saluti, quae cadunt sub praecepto vel prohibitione legis. Secundo, quia huiusmodi etiam praecepta vel prohibitiones facit nos libere implere, inquantum ex interiori instinctu gratiae ea implemus. Et propter haec duo lex nova dicitur lex perfectae libertatis, Ja 1)".

But this freedom is entirely at the service of love: "For you were called to freedom, brethren; only do not use your freedom as an opportunity for the flesh, but through love be servants of one another" (*Gal* 5:13).

112. The new law of the Gospel includes, assumes and fulfils the requirements of the natural law. The orientations of the natural law are not therefore external normative demands with respect to the new law. They are a constitutive part of it, even if they are secondary and completely ordered to the principal element, which is the grace of Christ[104]. Therefore, it is in the light of reason enlightened henceforth by living faith that man best grasps the orientations of natural law, which indicate to him the way to the full development of his humanity. Thus, the natural law, on the one hand, has "a fundamental link with the new law of the Spirit of life in Christ Jesus, and on the other hand, offers a broad basis for dialogue with persons who come from another cultural orientation or formation in the search for the common good"[105].

---

[104] St. Thomas Aquinas, *Quodlibeta*, IV, q. 8, a. 2: "The new law, which is the law of freedom, is constituted by the moral precepts of the natural law, by the articles of faith, and by the sacraments of grace (Lex nova, quae est lex libertatis, est contenta praeceptis moralibus naturalis legis, et articulis fidei, et sacramentis gratiae)".

[105] John Paul II, *Address of January 18, 2002* (AAS 94 [2002], p. 334).

CONCLUSION

113. The Catholic Church, aware of the need for human beings to seek in common the rules for living together in justice and peace, desires to share with the religions, wisdoms and philosophies of our time the resources of the concept of natural law. We call natural law the foundation of a universal ethic which we seek to draw from the observation of and reflection on our common human nature. It is the moral law inscribed in the heart of human beings and of which humanity becomes ever more aware as it advances in history. This natural law is not at all static in its expression. It does not consist of a list of definitive and immutable precepts. It is a spring of inspiration always flowing forth for the search for an objective foundation for a universal ethic.

114. Our conviction of faith is that Christ reveals the fullness of what is human by realizing it in his person. But this revelation, specific as it may be, brings together and confirms elements already present in the rational thought of the wisdom traditions of humanity. The concept of natural law is first of all philosophical, and as such, it allows a dialog that, always respecting the religious convictions of each, appeals to what is universally human in every human being. An exchange on the level of reason is possible when it is a question of experiencing and expressing what is common to all persons endowed with reason, and of setting out the requirements of life in society.

115. The discovery of natural law responds to the quest of a humanity that from time immemorial always seeks to give itself rules for moral life and life in society. This life in society regards a whole spectrum of relations that reach from the family unit to international relations, passing through economic life, civil society, and the political community. To be able to be recognized by all persons and in all cultures, the norms of behaviour in society should have their source in the human person himself, in his needs, in his inclinations. These norms, elaborated by reflection and upheld by law, can thus be interiorized by all. After the Second World War, the nations of the entire world were able to create a *Universal Declaration of Human Rights*, which implicitly suggests that the source of inalienable human rights is found in the dignity of every human person. The present

contribution has no other aim than that of helping to reflect on this source of personal and collective morality.

116. In offering our own contribution to the search for a universal ethic and in proposing a rationally justifiable basis for it, we want to invite the experts and proponents of the great religious, sapiential and philosophical traditions of humanity to undertake an analogous work, beginning from their own sources, in order to reach a common recognition of universal moral norms based on a rational approach to reality. This work is necessary and urgent. Beyond the differences of our religious convictions and the diversity of our cultural presuppositions, we must be capable of expressing the fundamental values of our common humanity, in order to work together for understanding, mutual recognition and peaceful cooperation among all the members of the human family.

NOTES

* PRELIMINARY NOTE.

The topic "In Search of a Universal Ethic: A New Look at the Natural Law" was submitted to the study of the International Theological Commission. To undertake this study a Subcommittee was formed, composed of Archbishop Roland Minnerath, the Reverend Professors: P. Serge-Thomas Bonino OP (Chairman of the Subcommittee), Geraldo Luis Borges Hackmann, Pierre Gaudette, Tony Kelly CSSR, Jean Liesen, John Michael McDermott SJ; Professors Dr. Johannes Reiter and Dr. Barbara Hallensleben, with the collaboration of Archbishop Luis Ladaria SJ, Secretary General, and with the contributions of other members. The general discussion took place on the occasion of the plenary sessions of the International Theological Commission, which took place in Rome in October 2006 and 2007 and in December 2008. The document was approved unanimously by the Commission and was then submitted to its president, Cardinal William J. Levada, who has given his approval for publication.